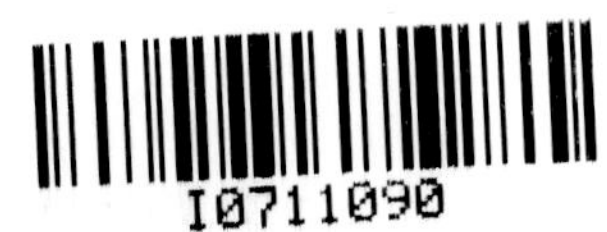

# THIS DINOSAUR COLORING BOOK

BELONGS TO:

_______________________

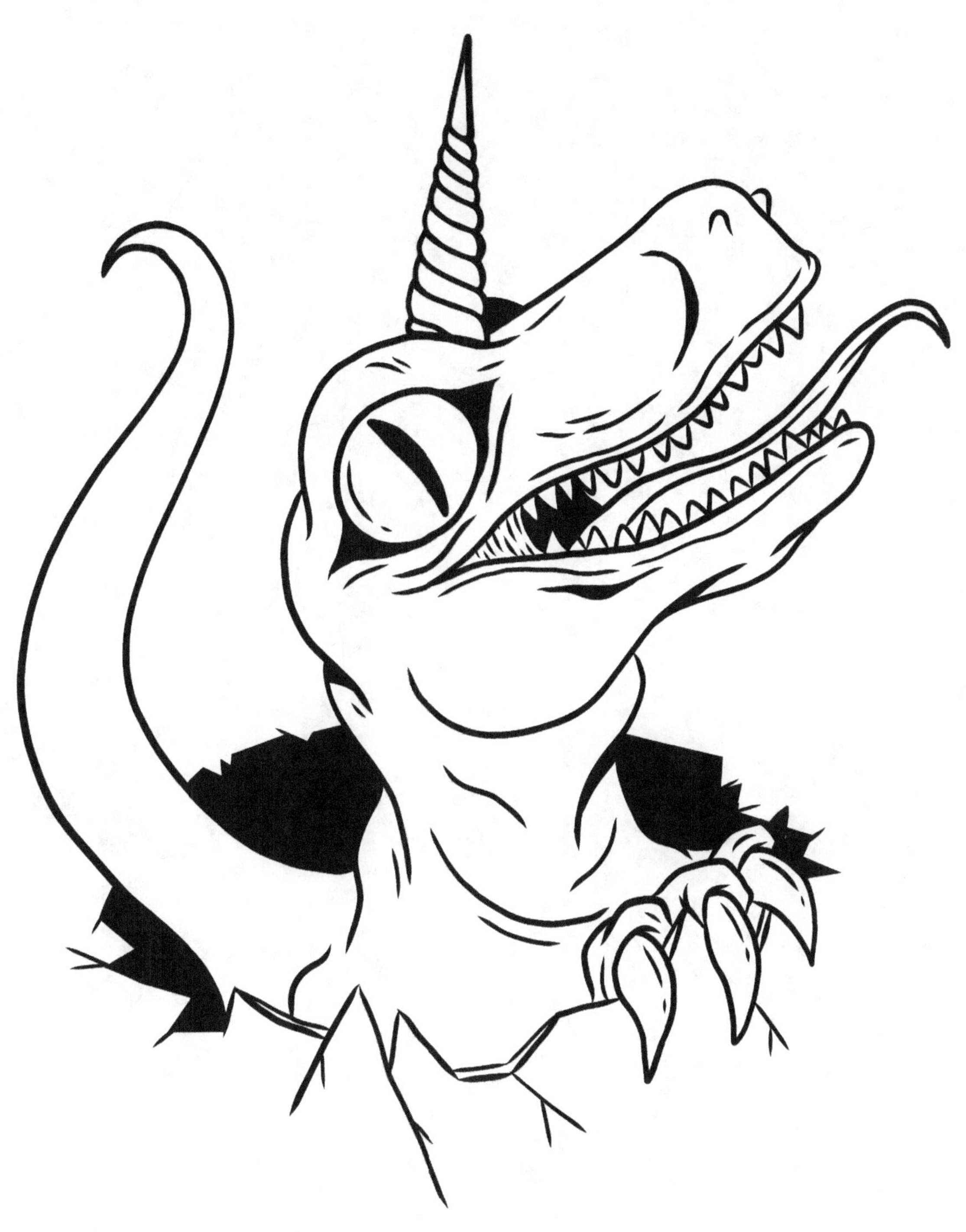

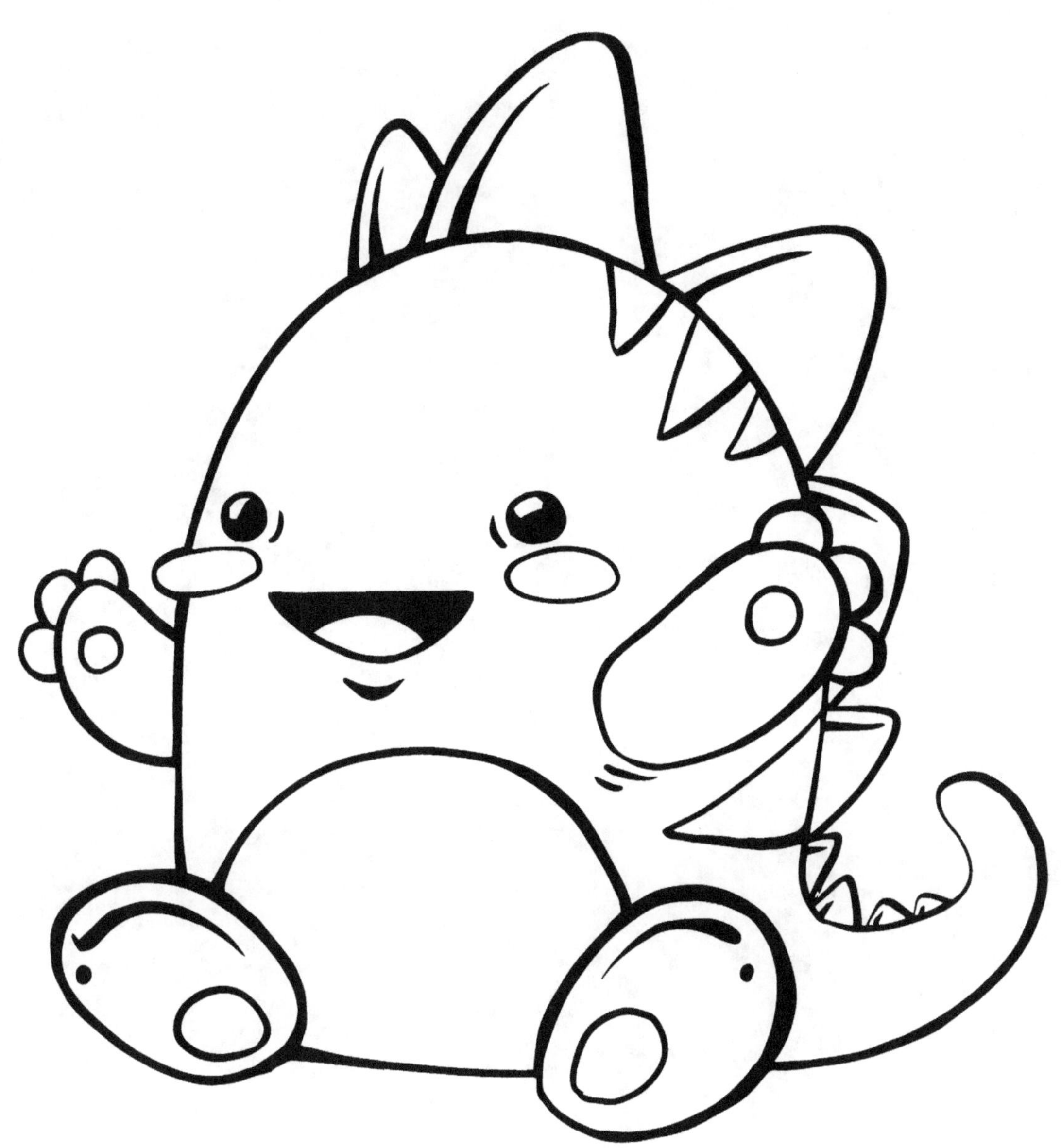

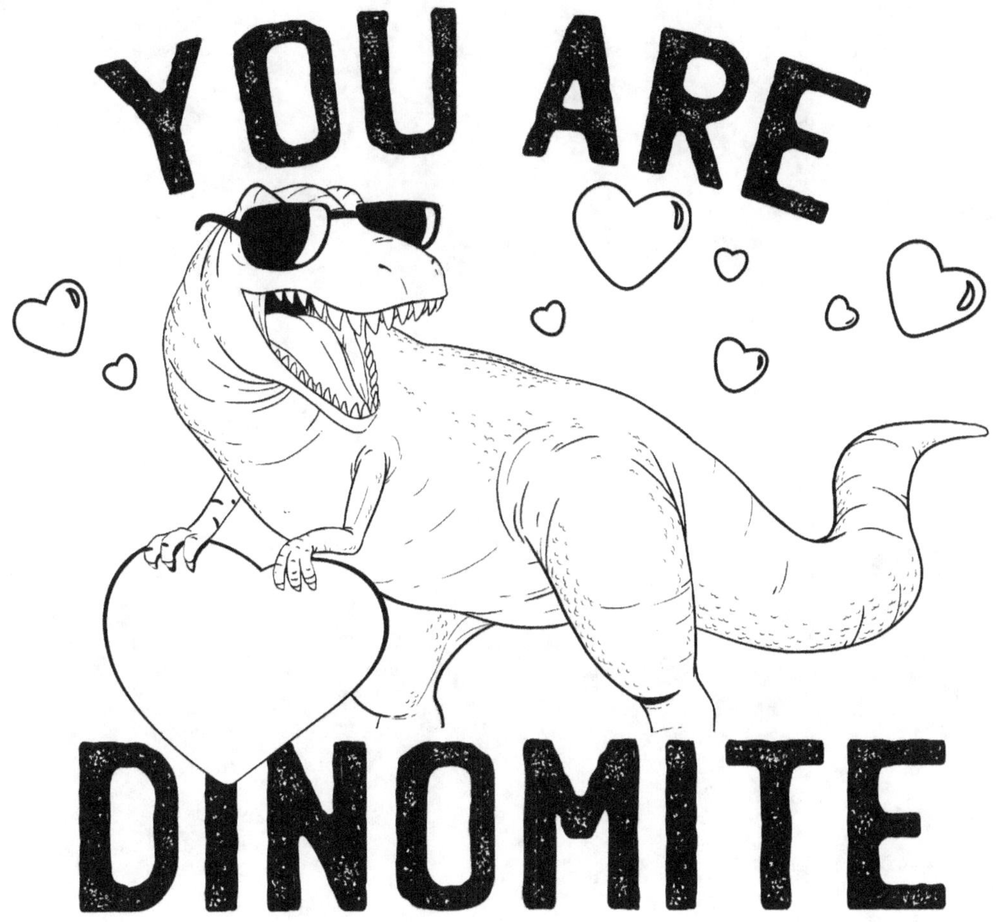

YOU ARE
DINOMITE

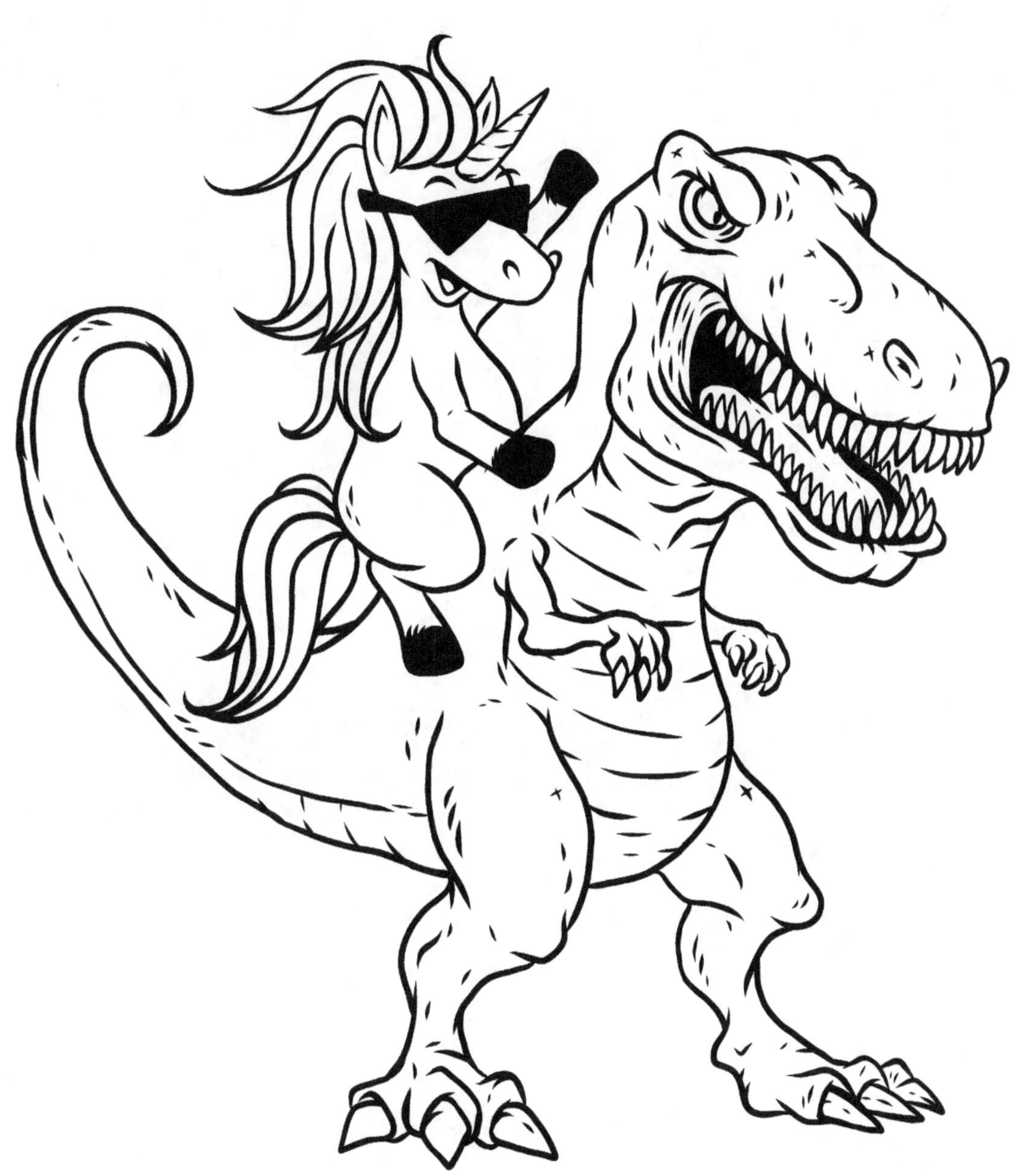

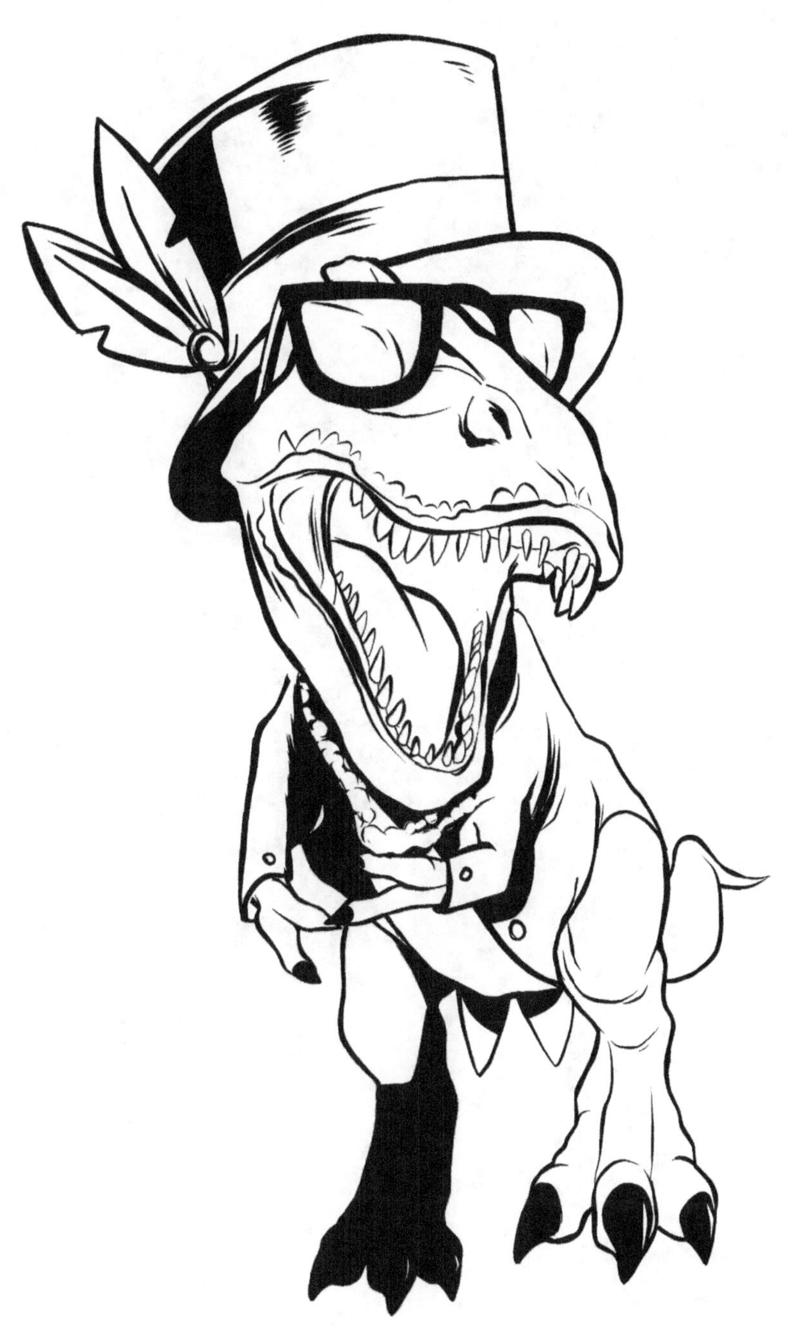

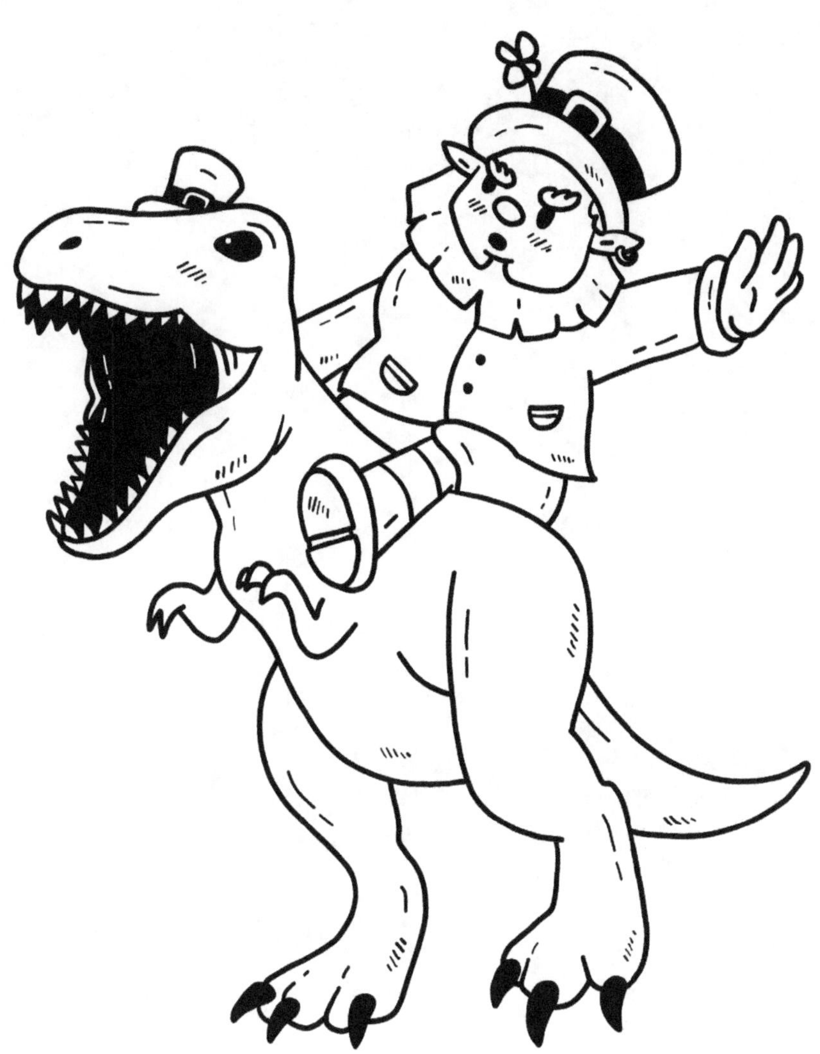

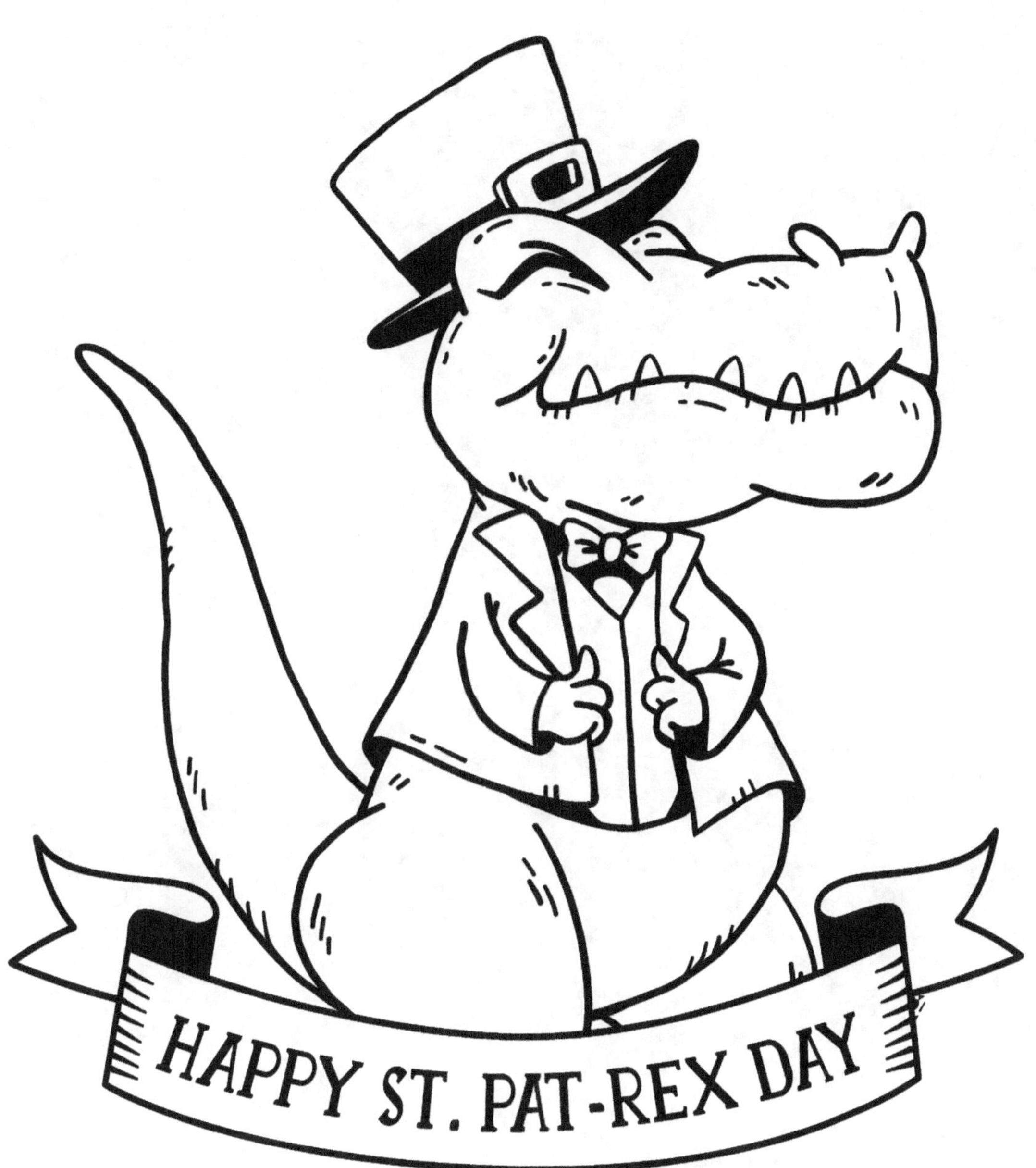

HAPPY ST. PAT-REX DAY

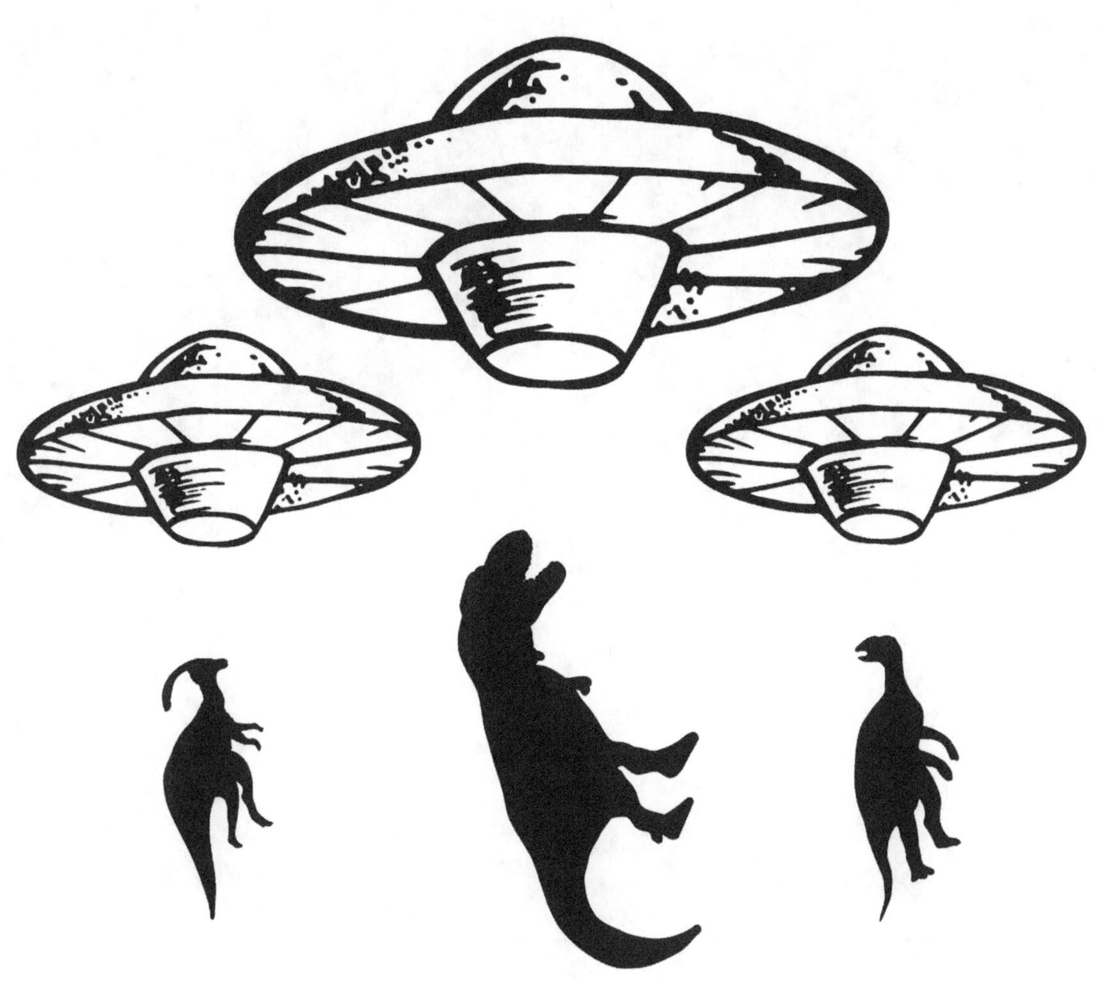

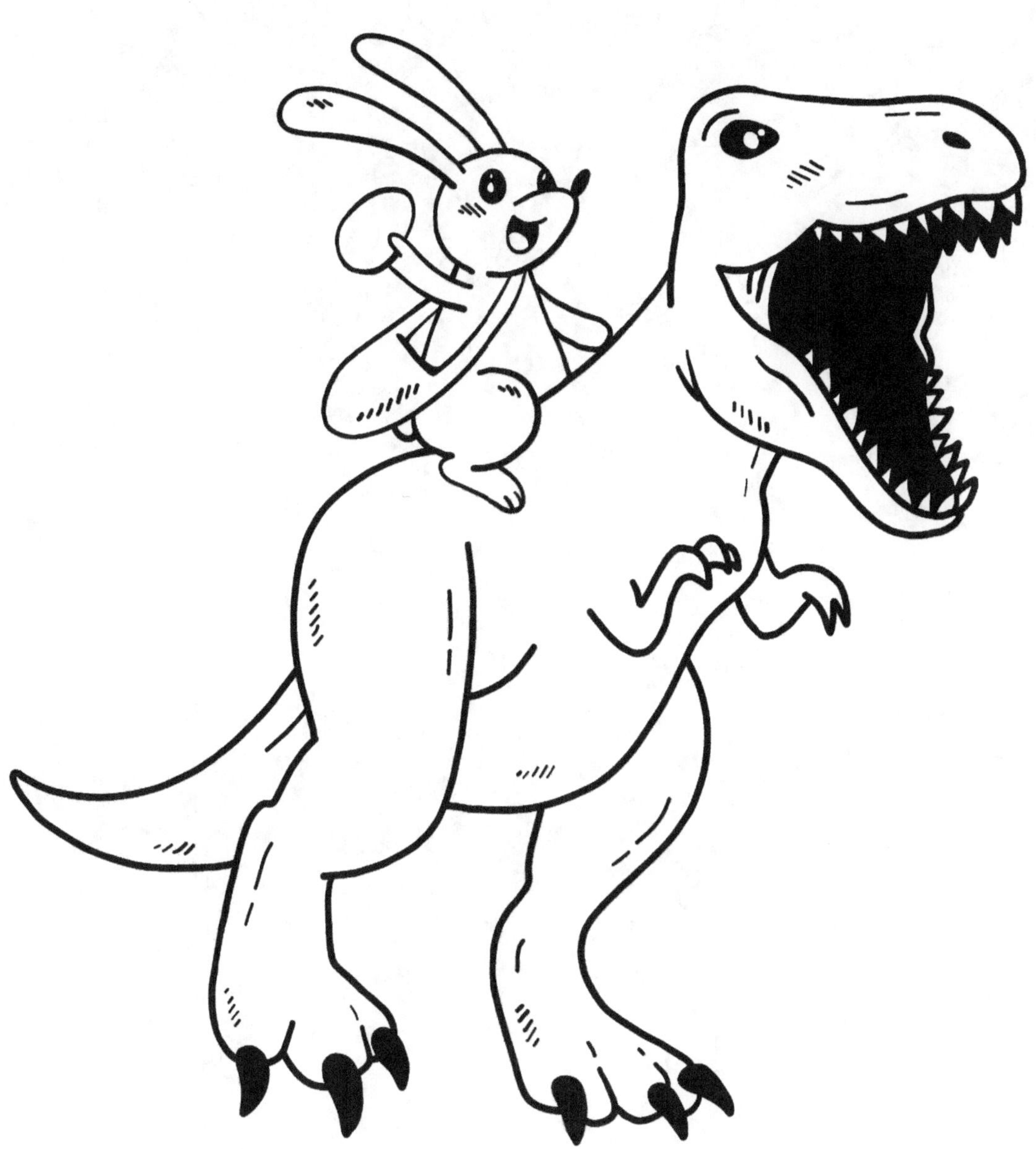

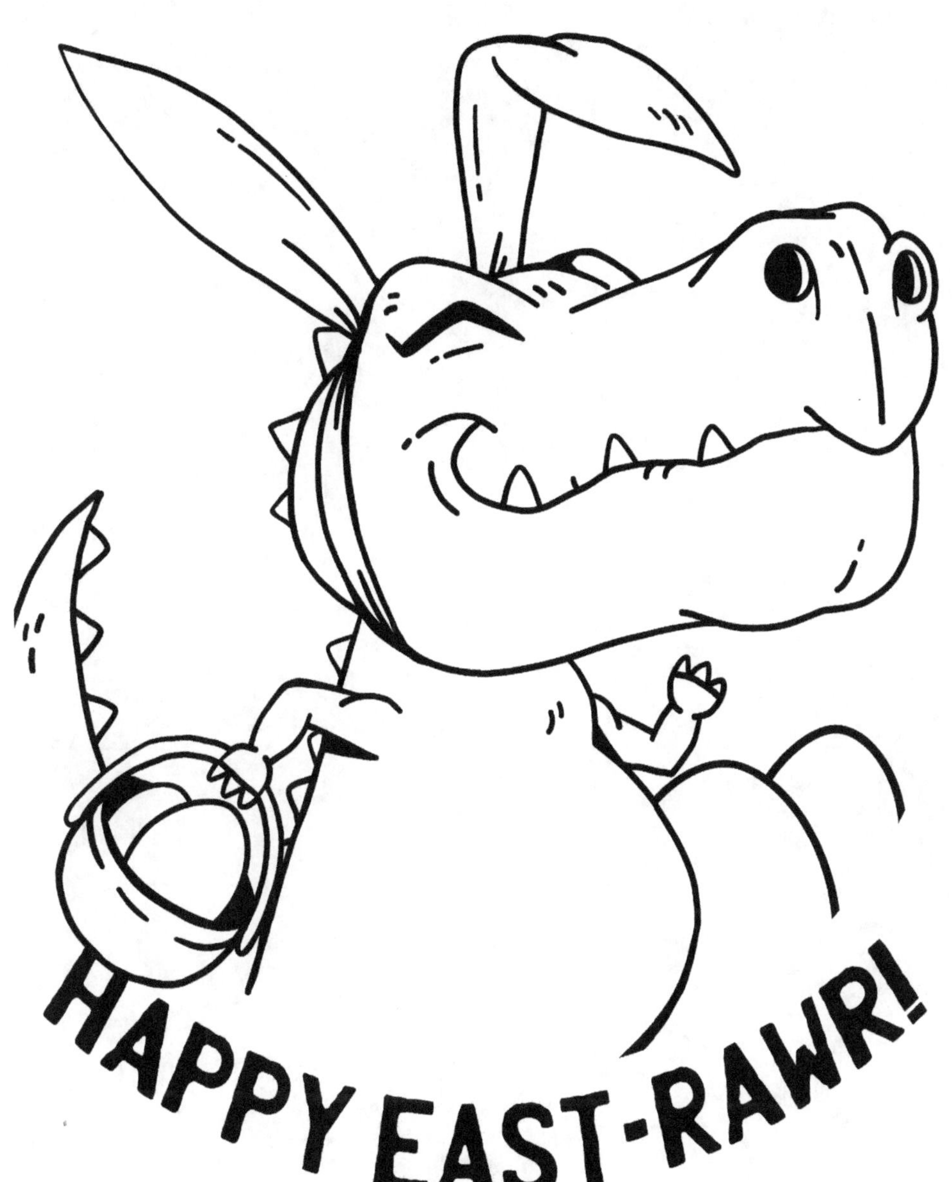
HAPPY EAST-RAWR!

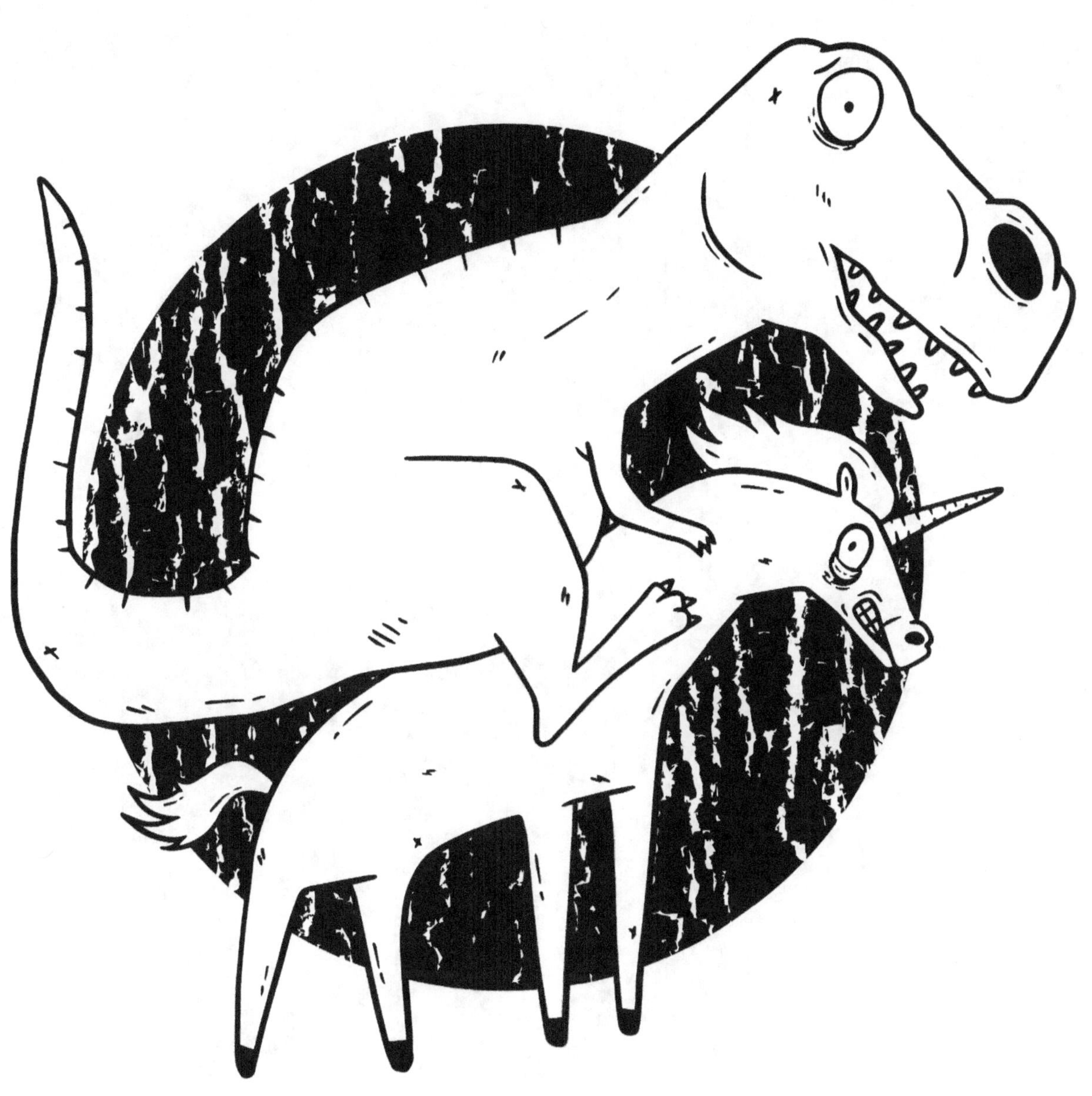

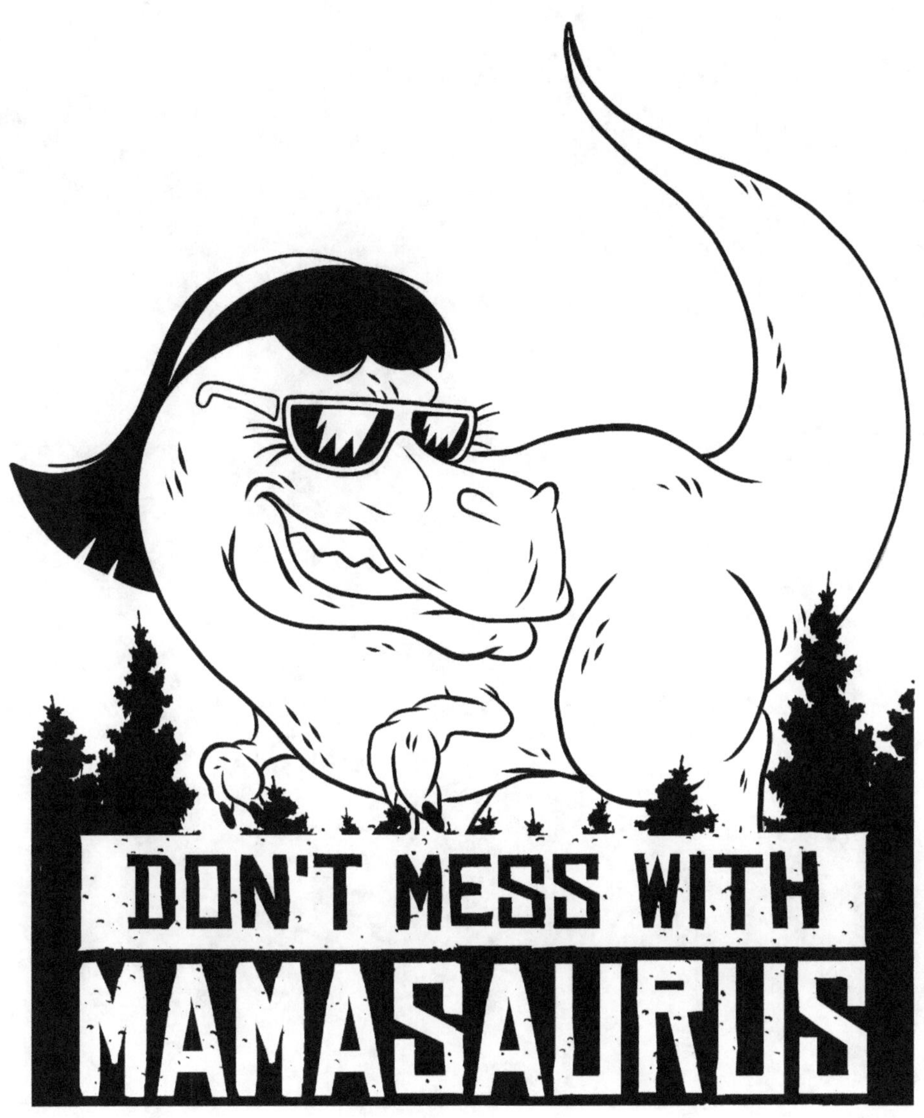
DON'T MESS WITH
MAMASAURUS

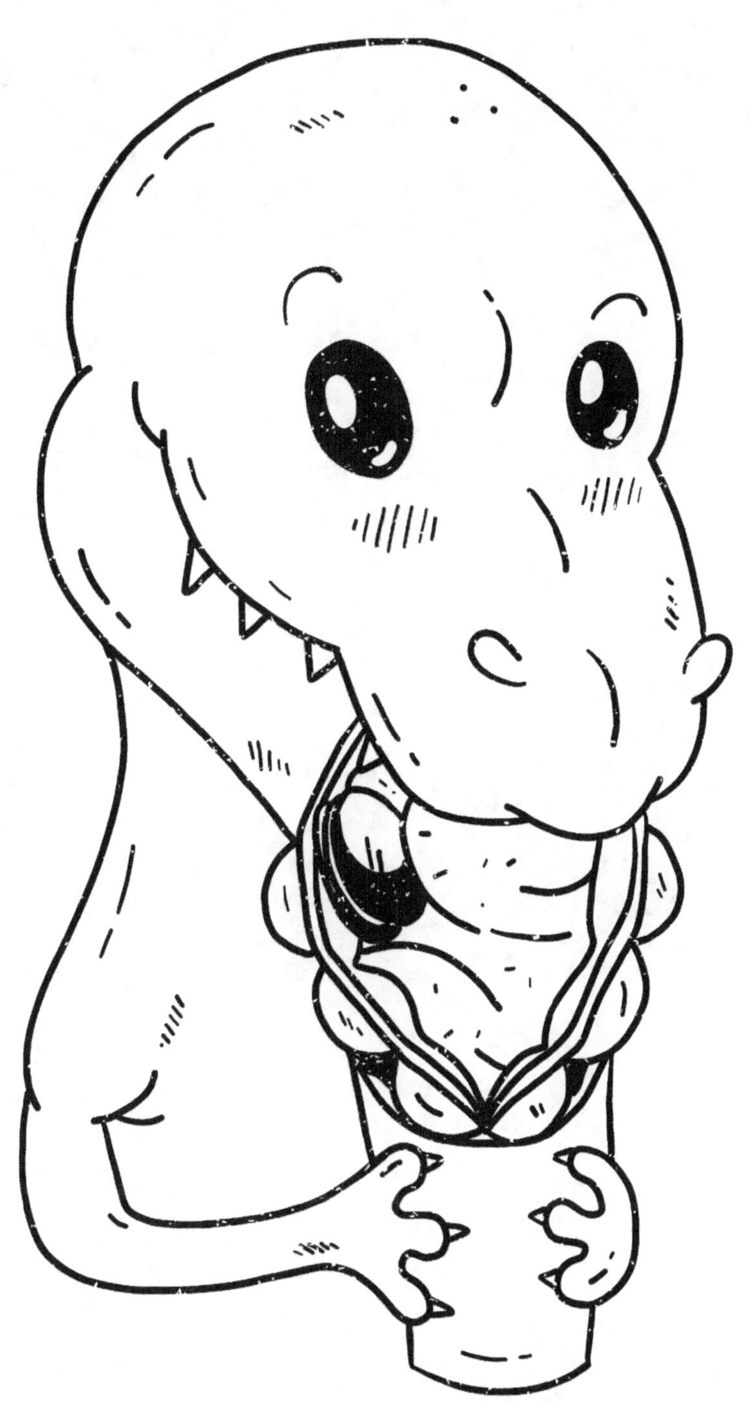

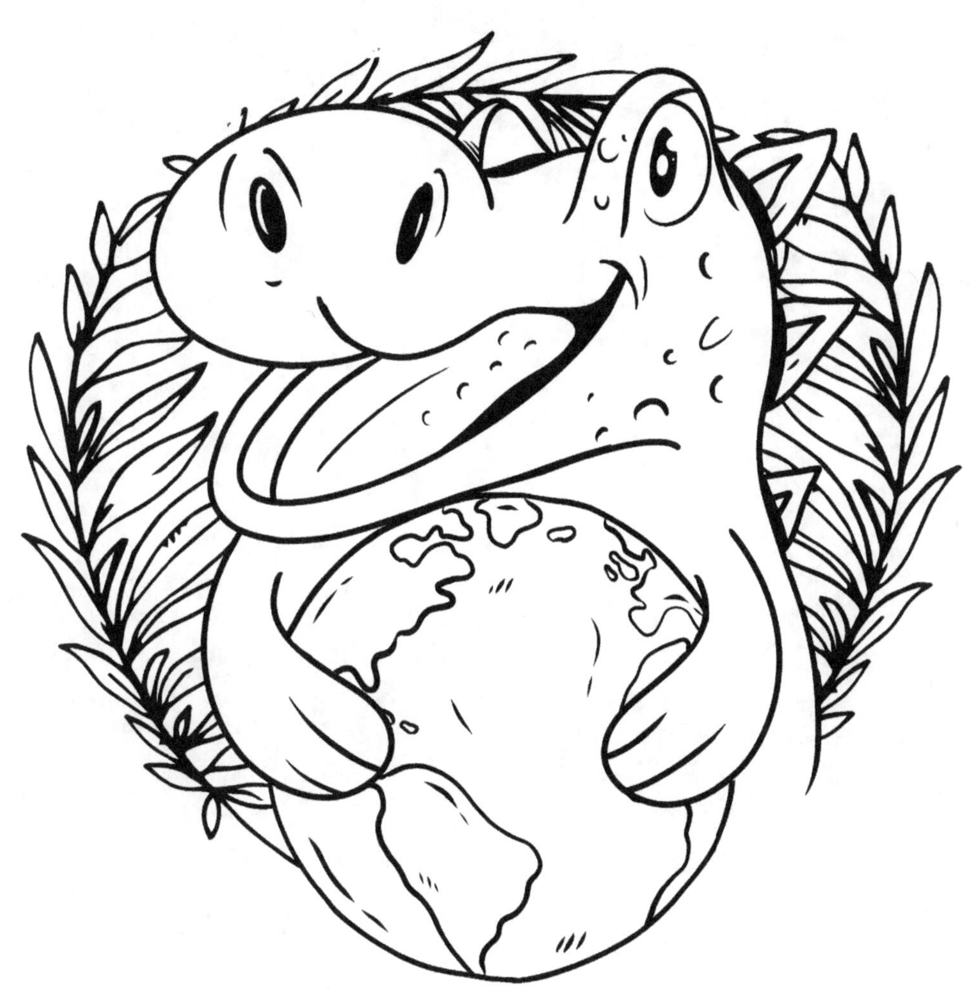

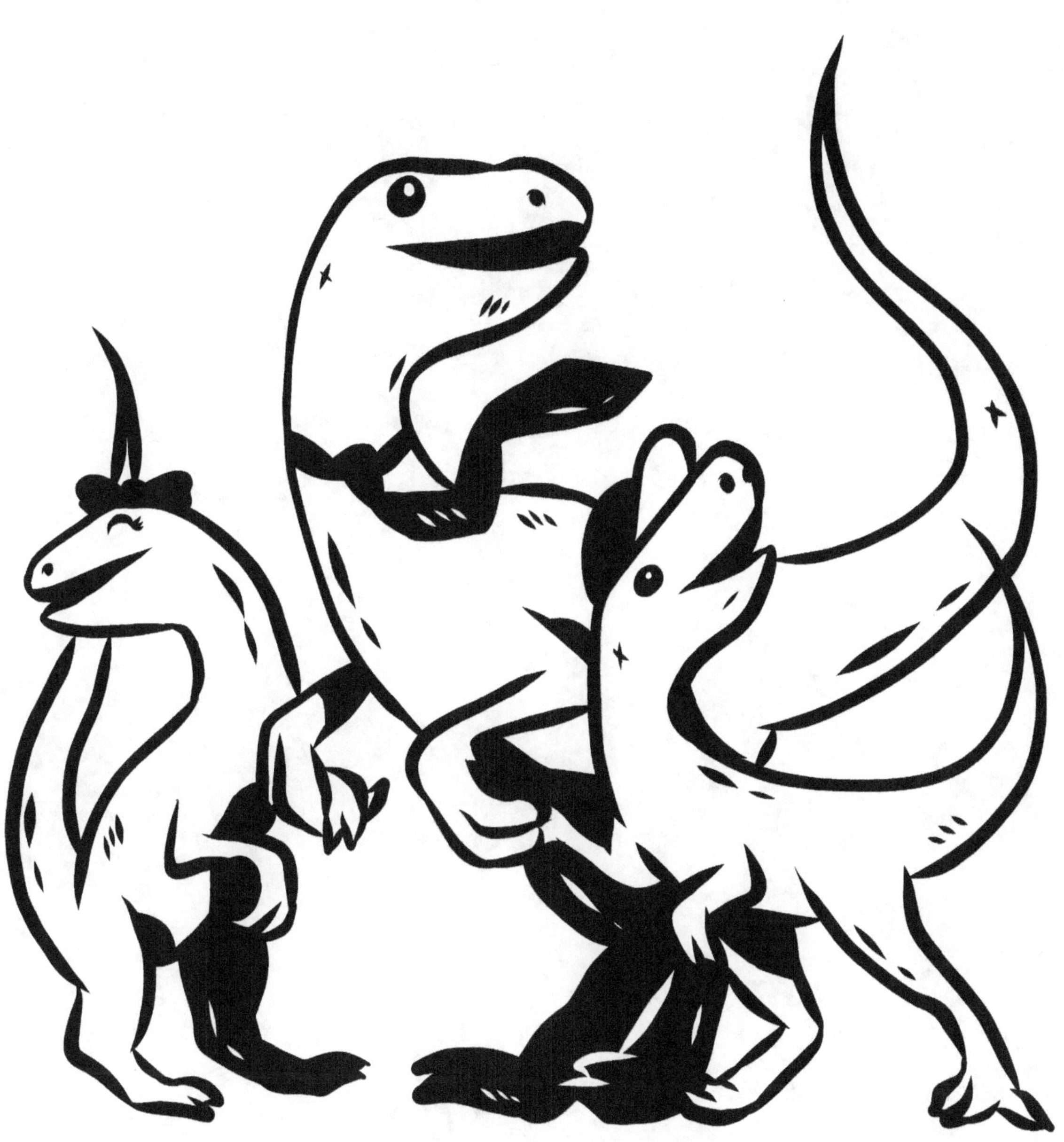

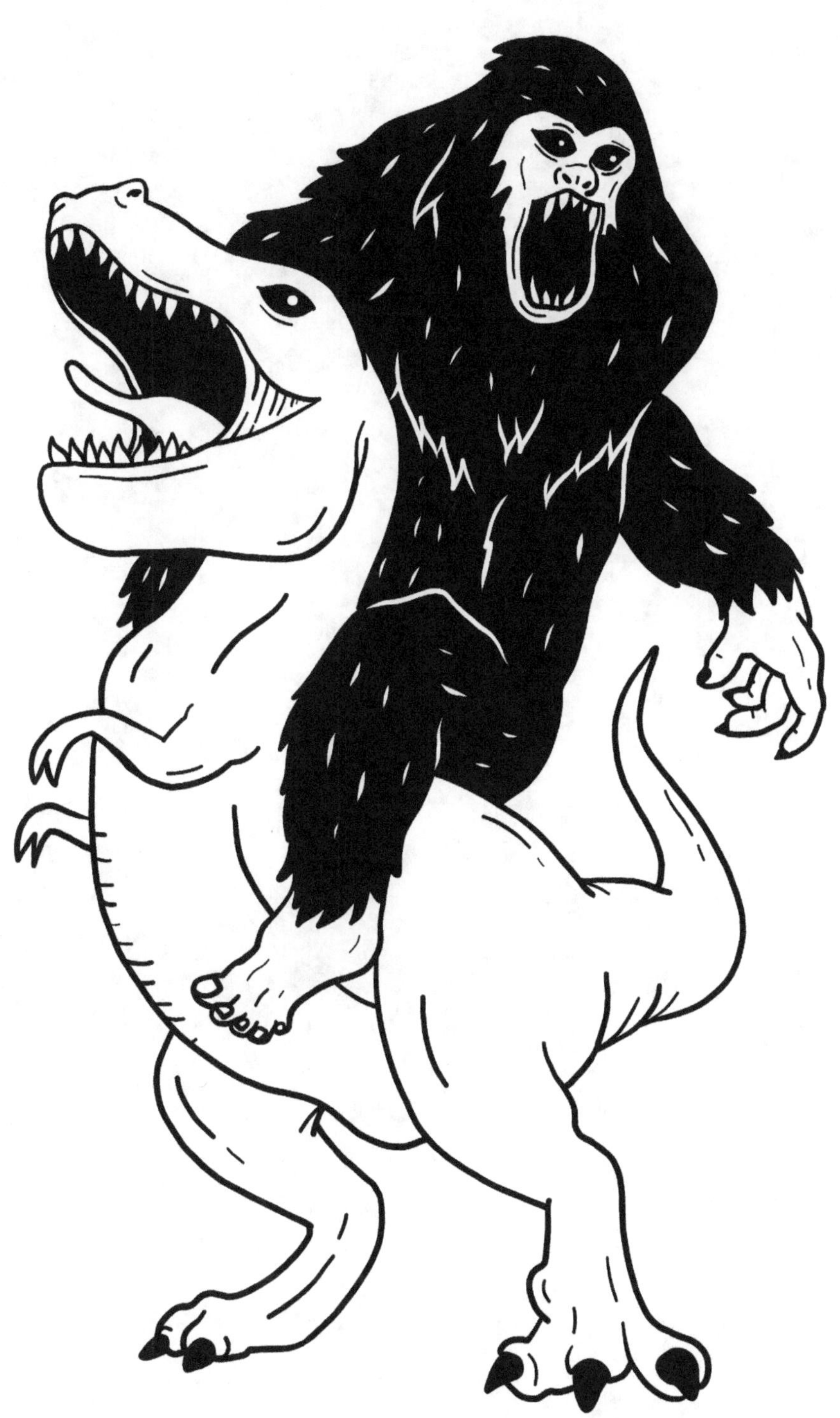

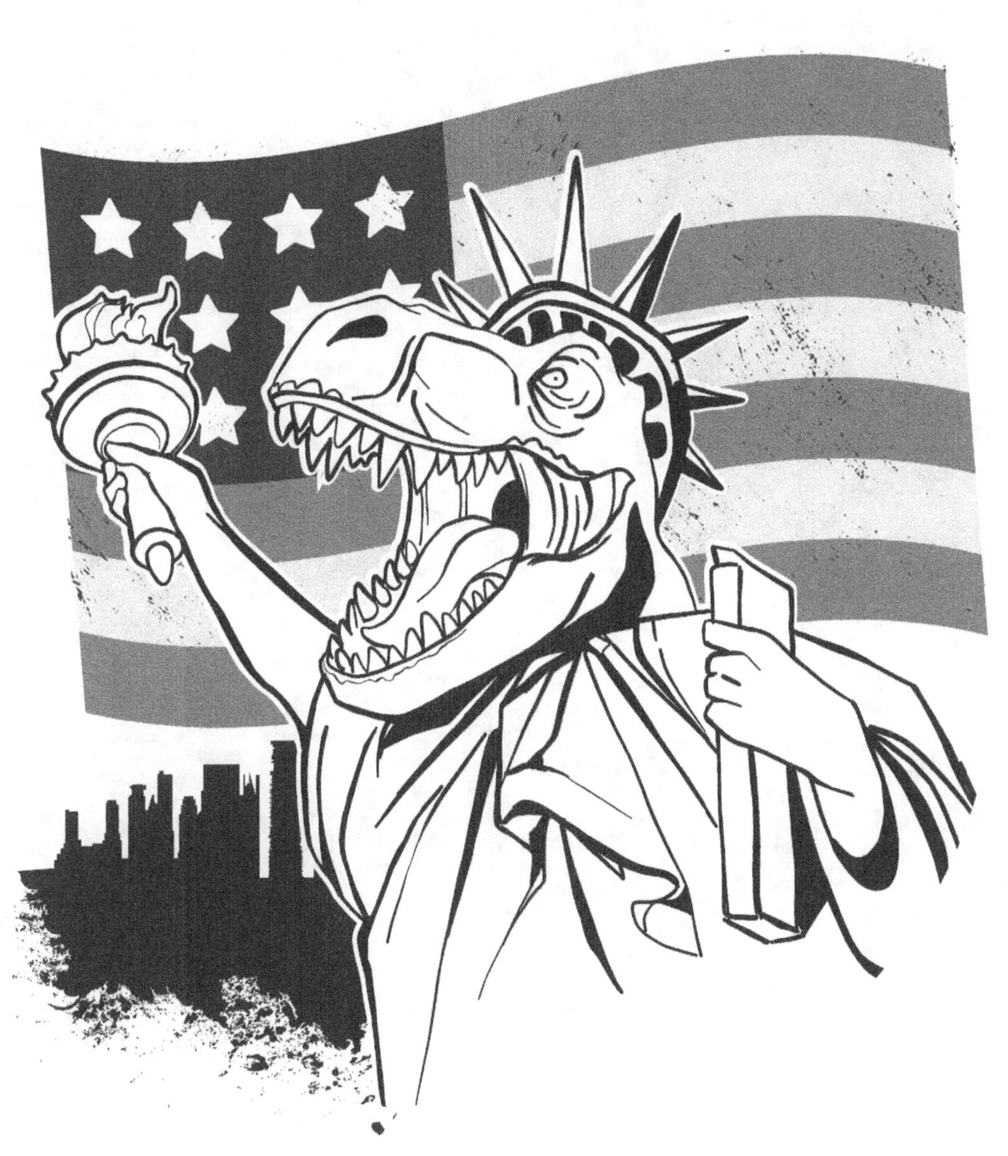

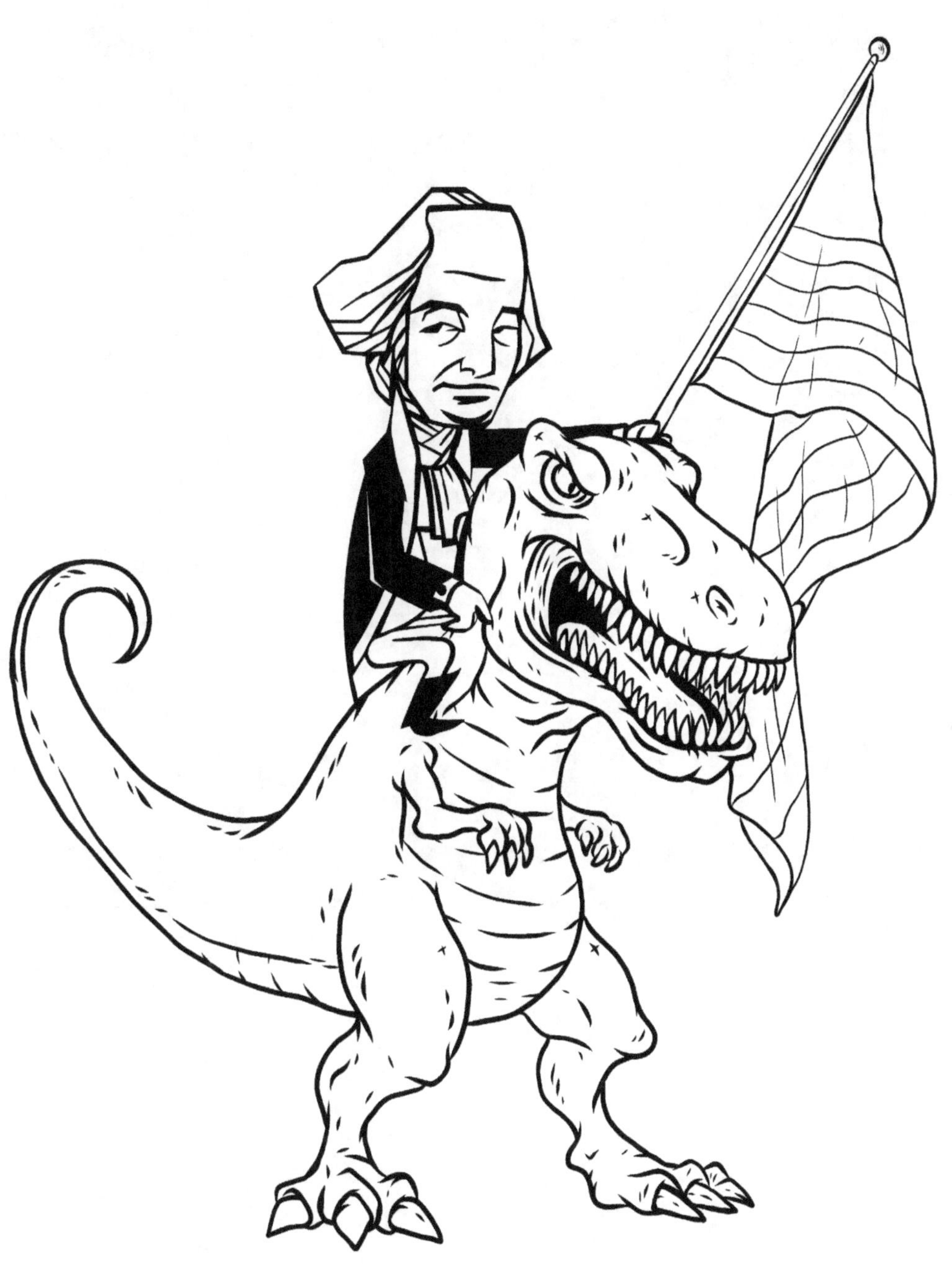

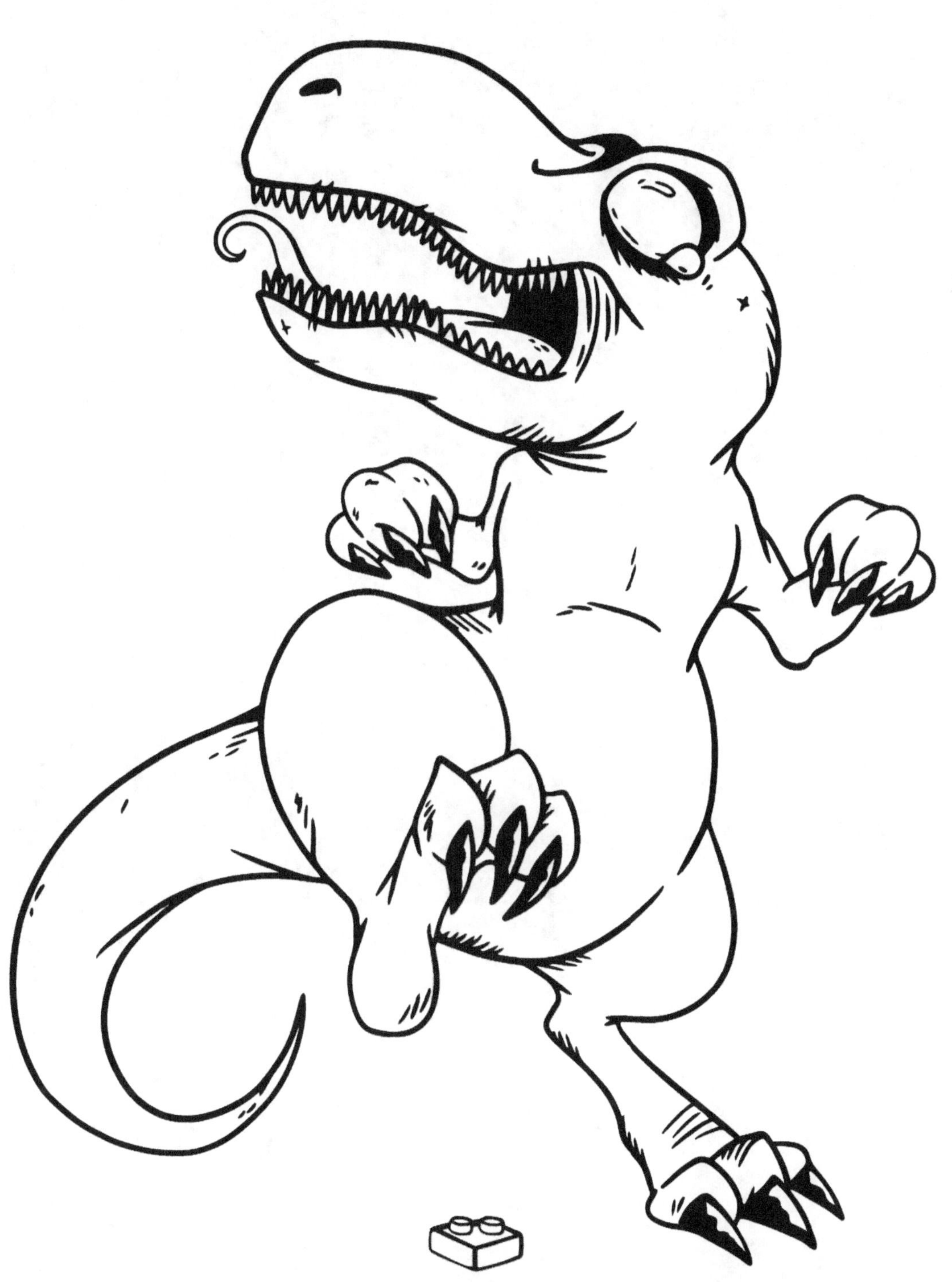

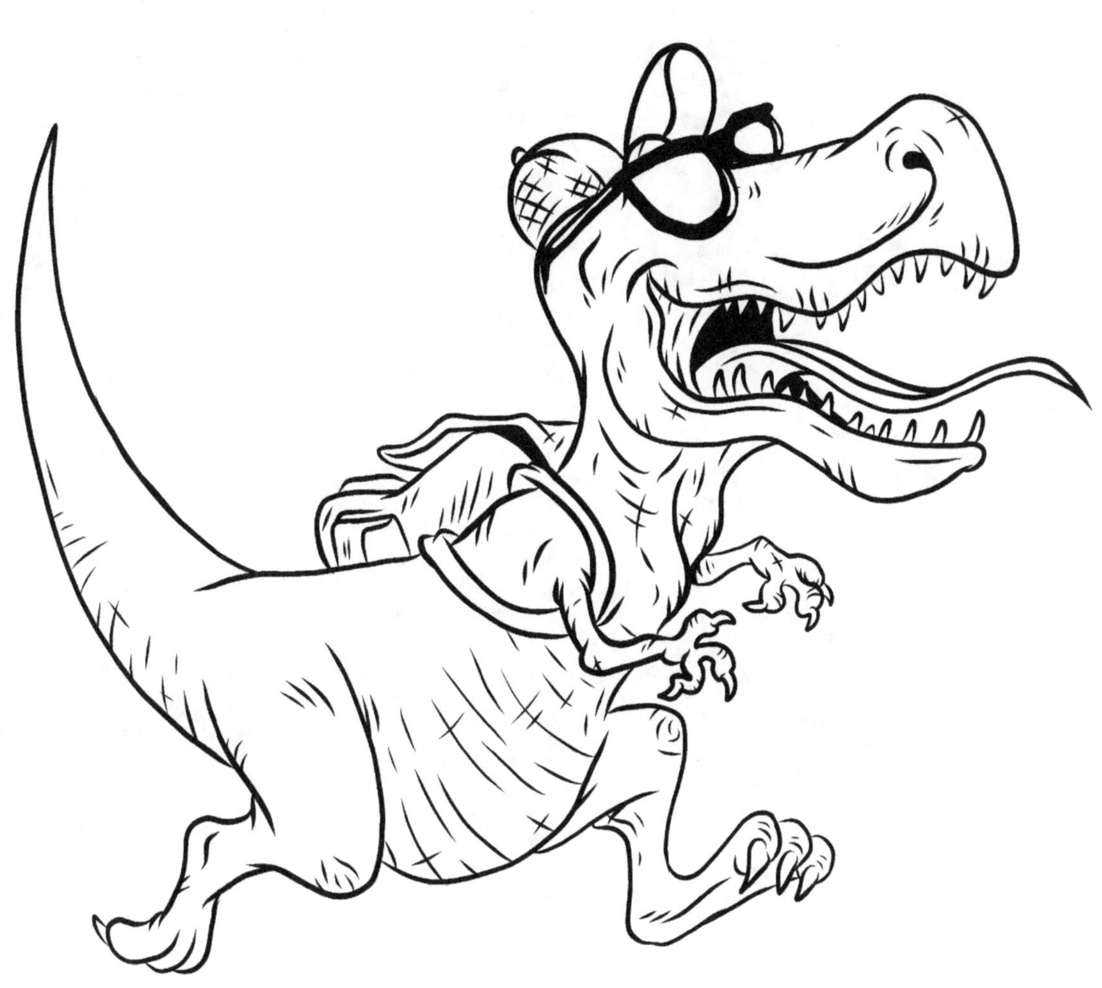

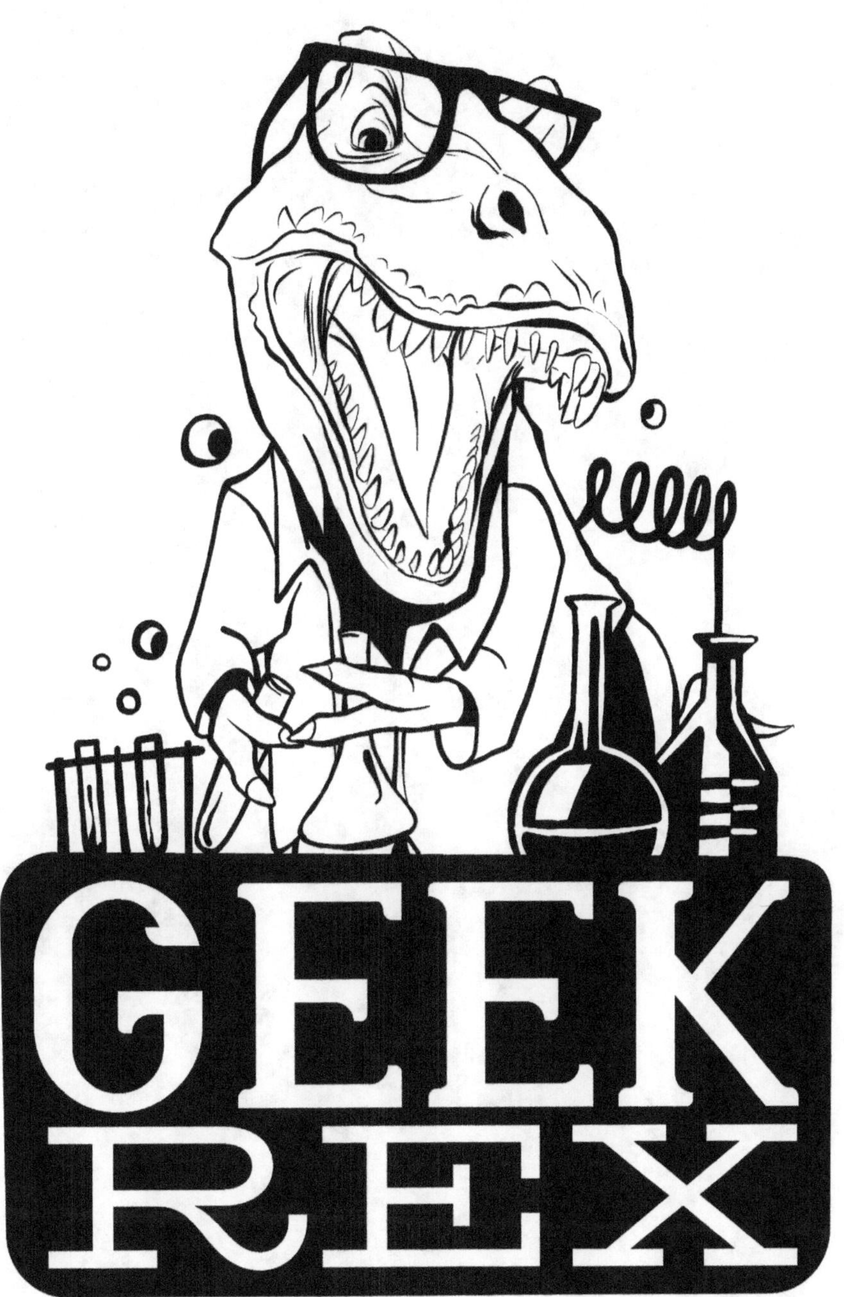
GEEK
REX

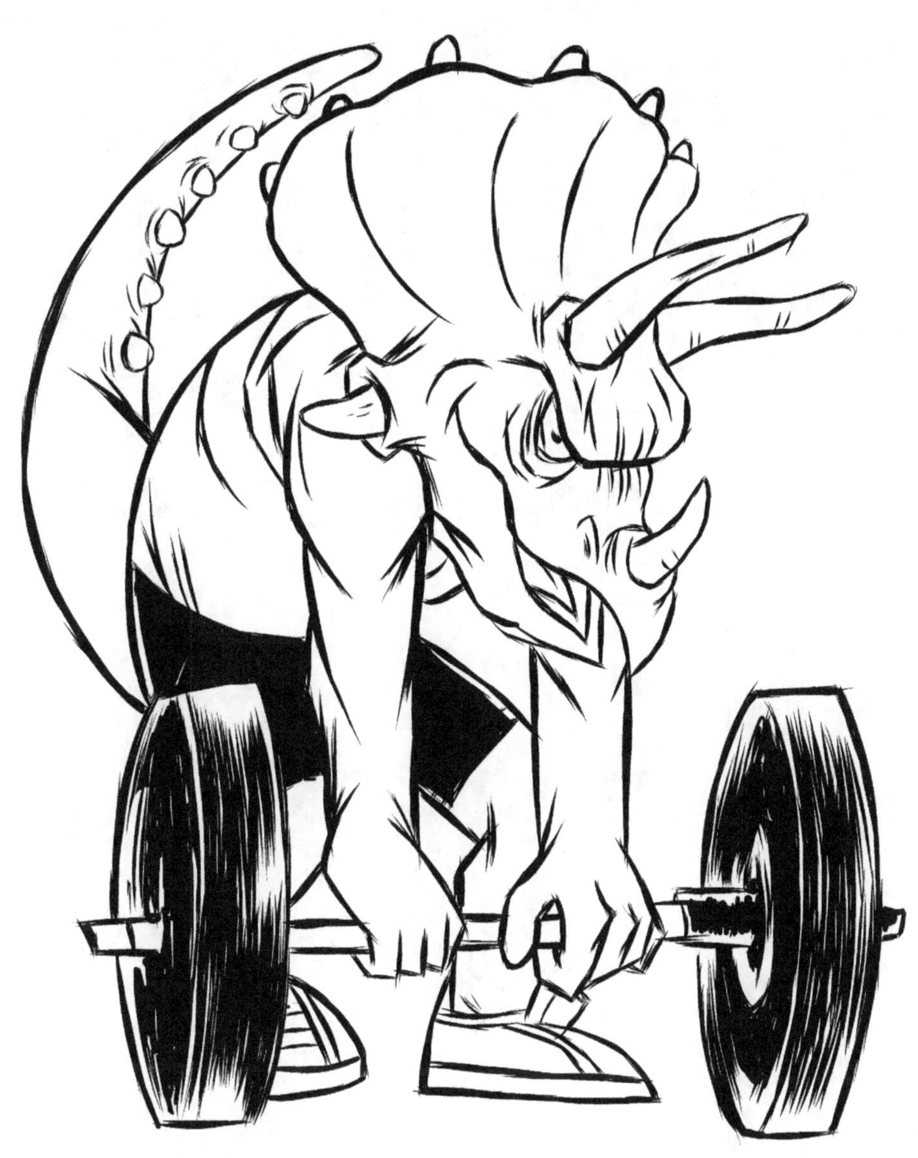

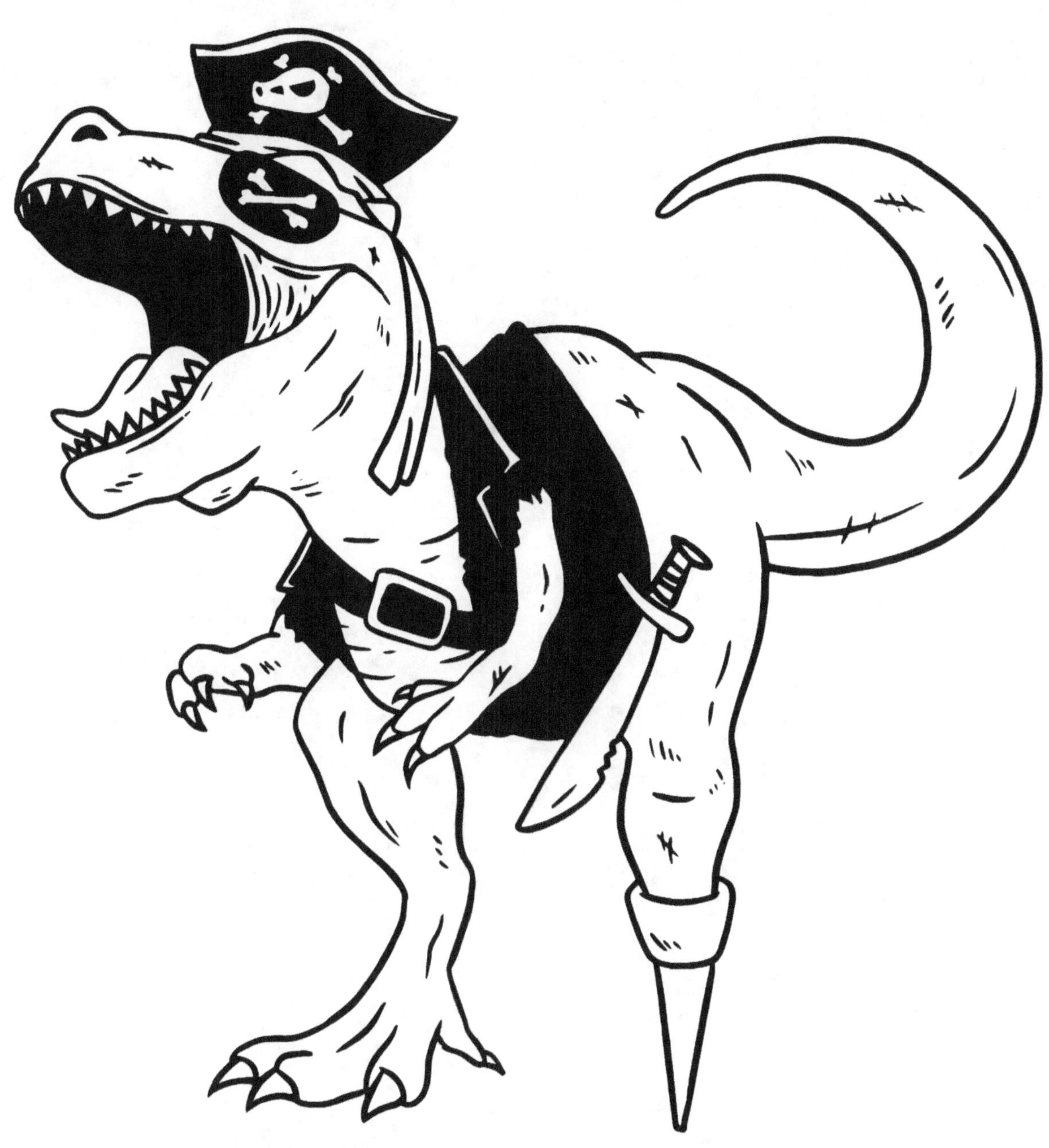

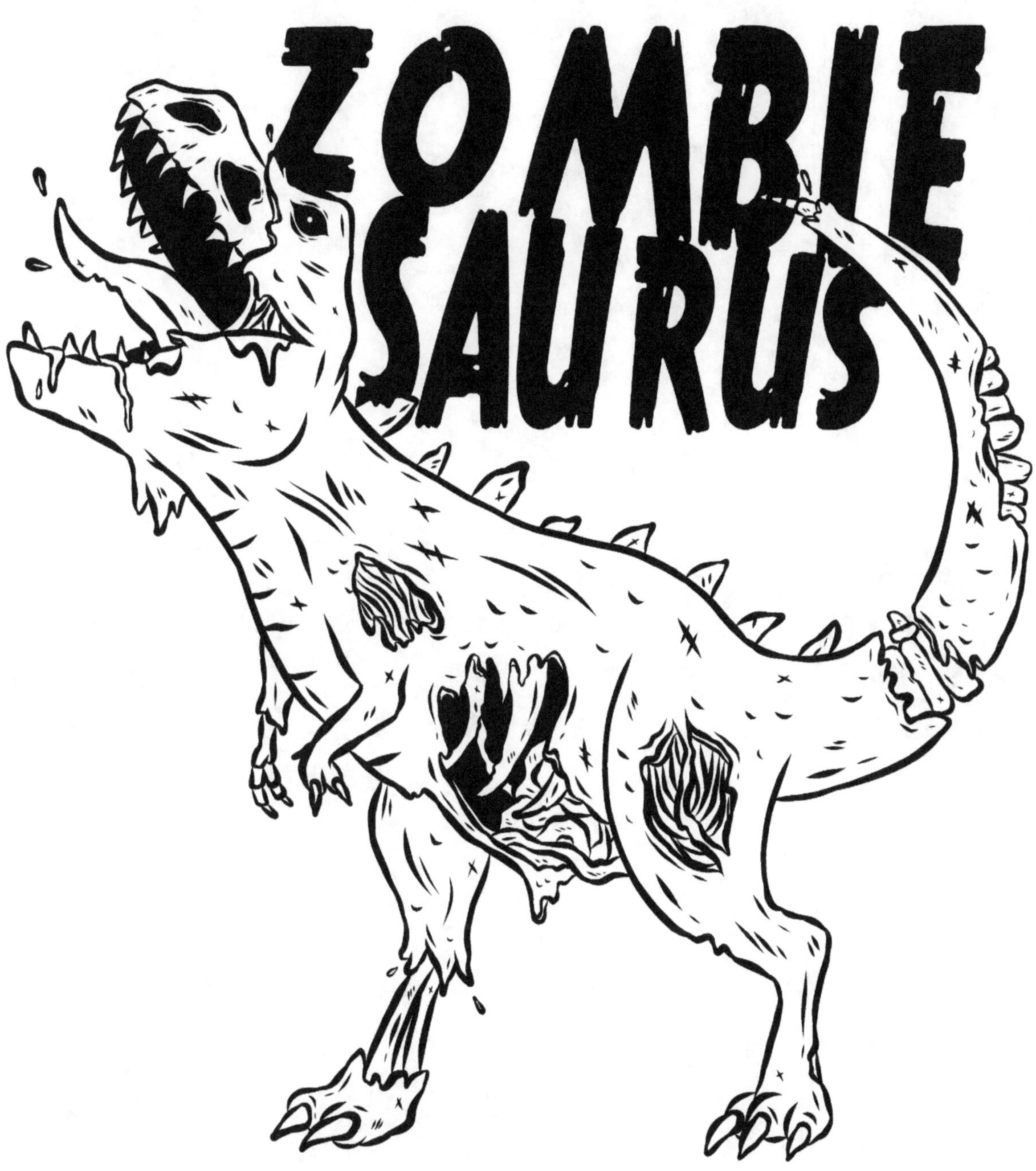

ZOMBIE
SAURUS

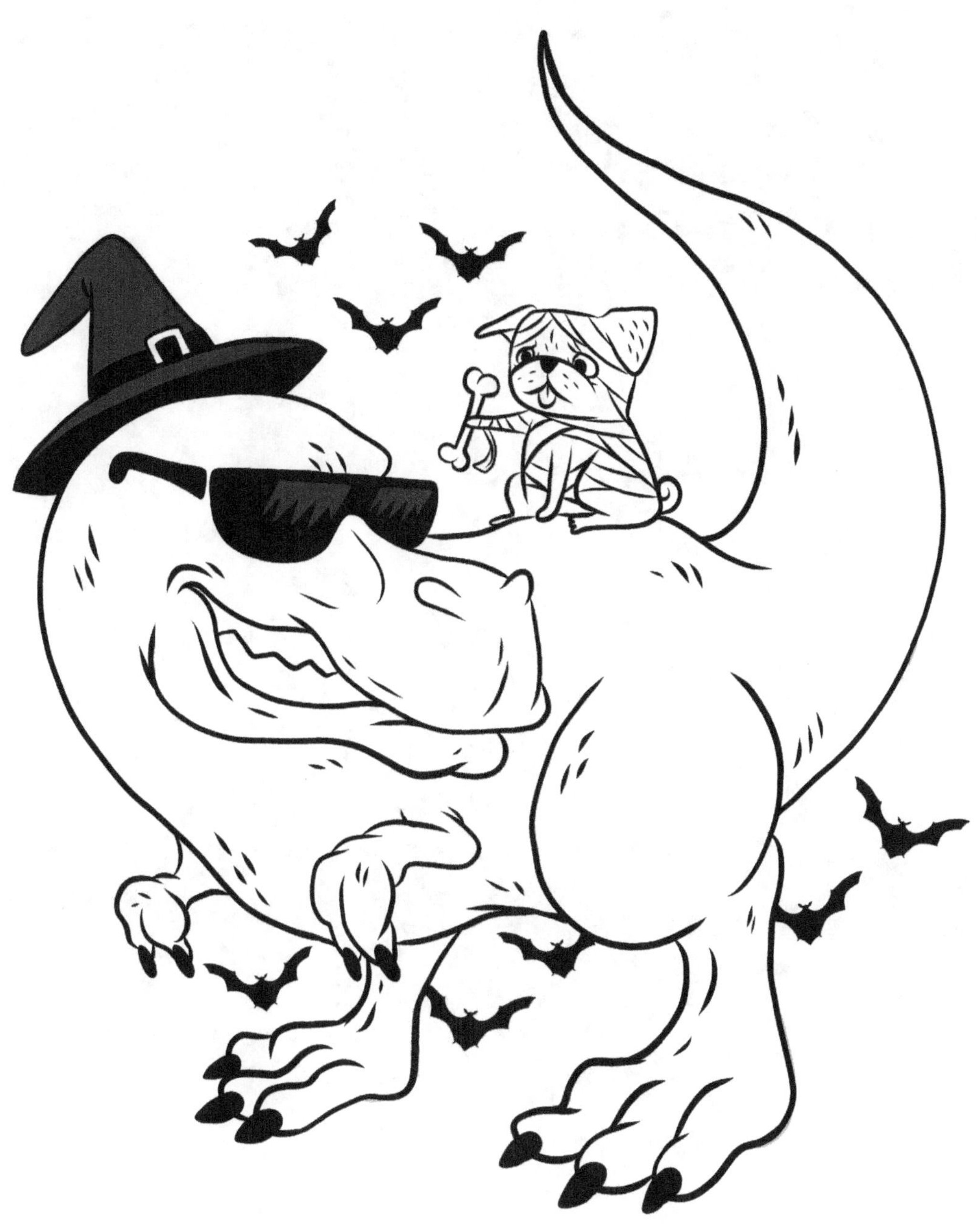

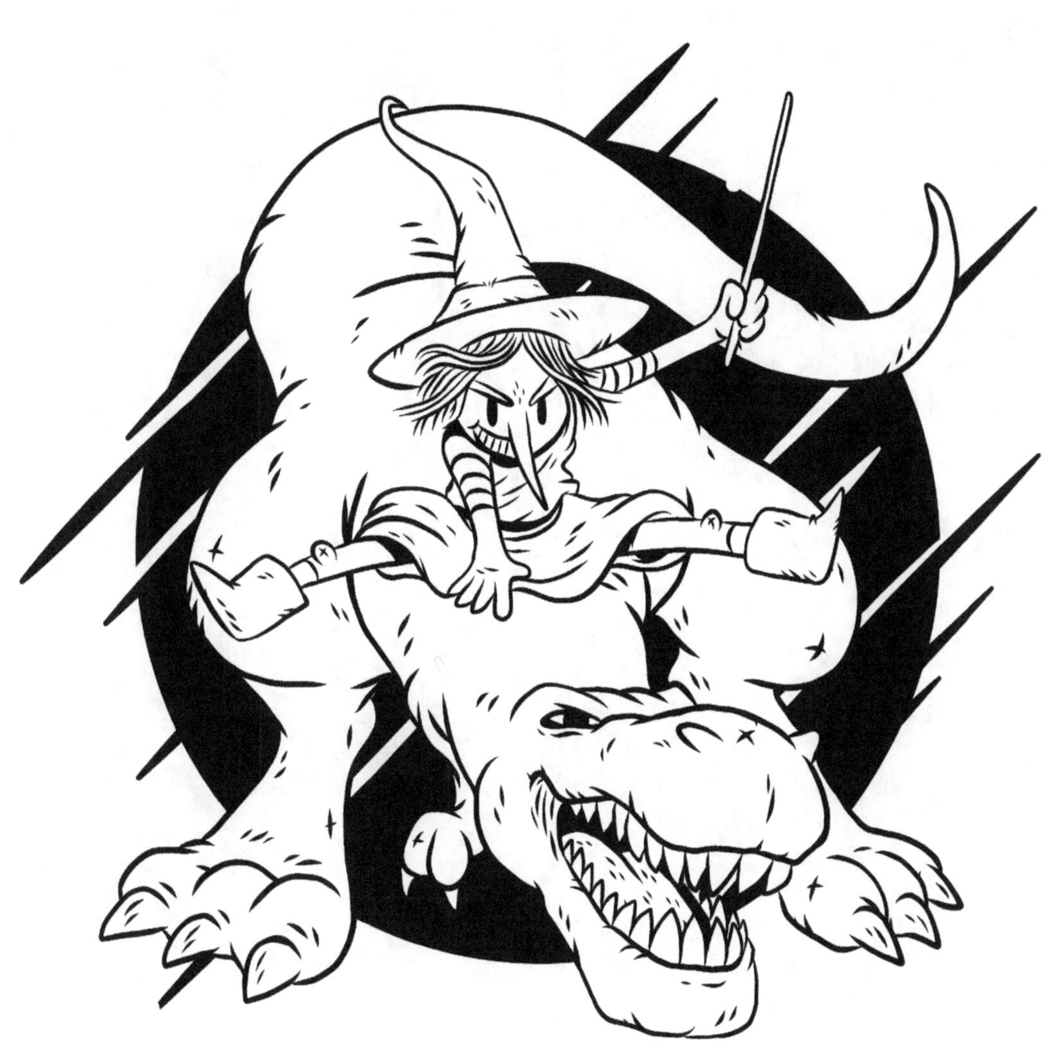

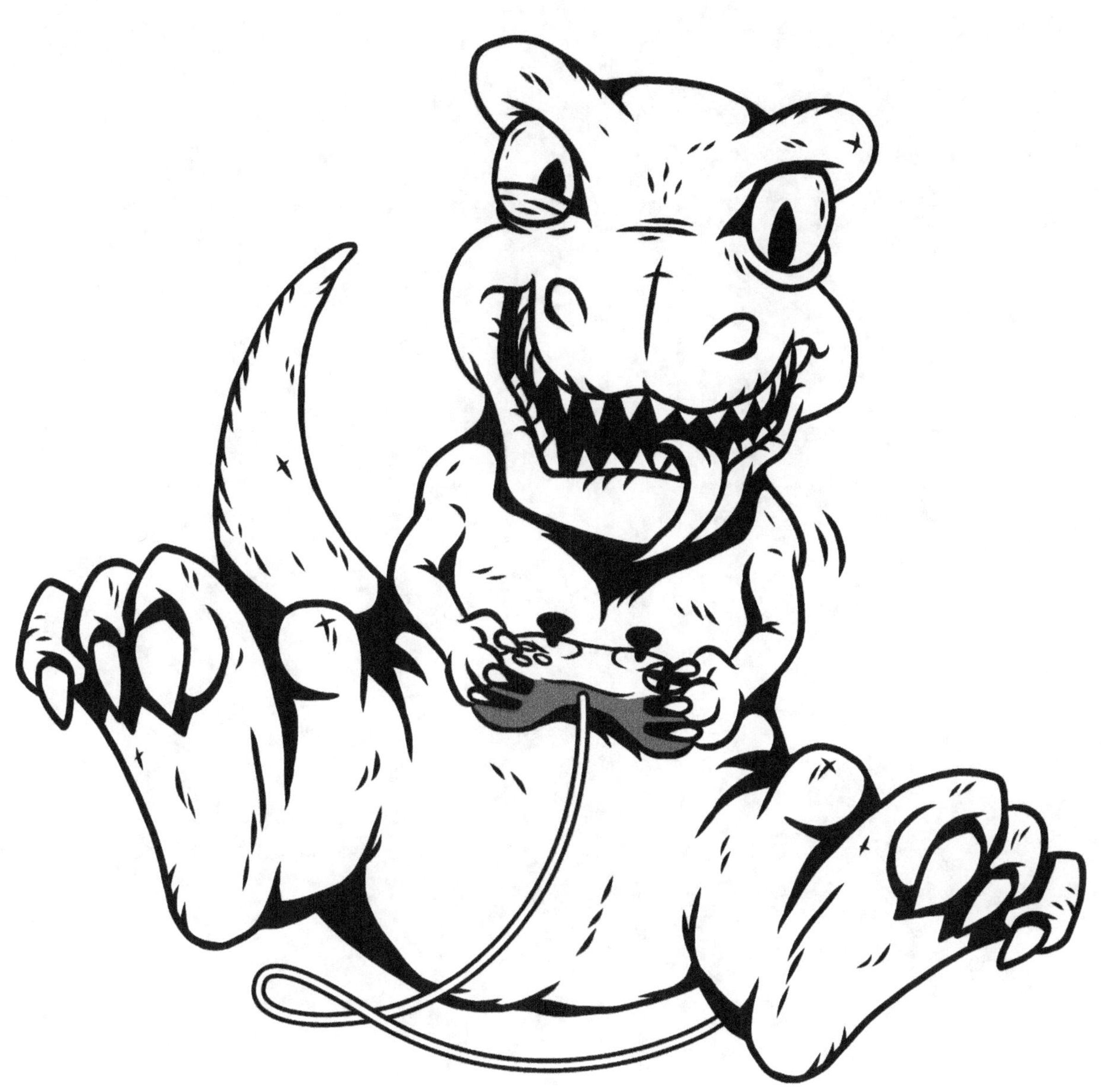

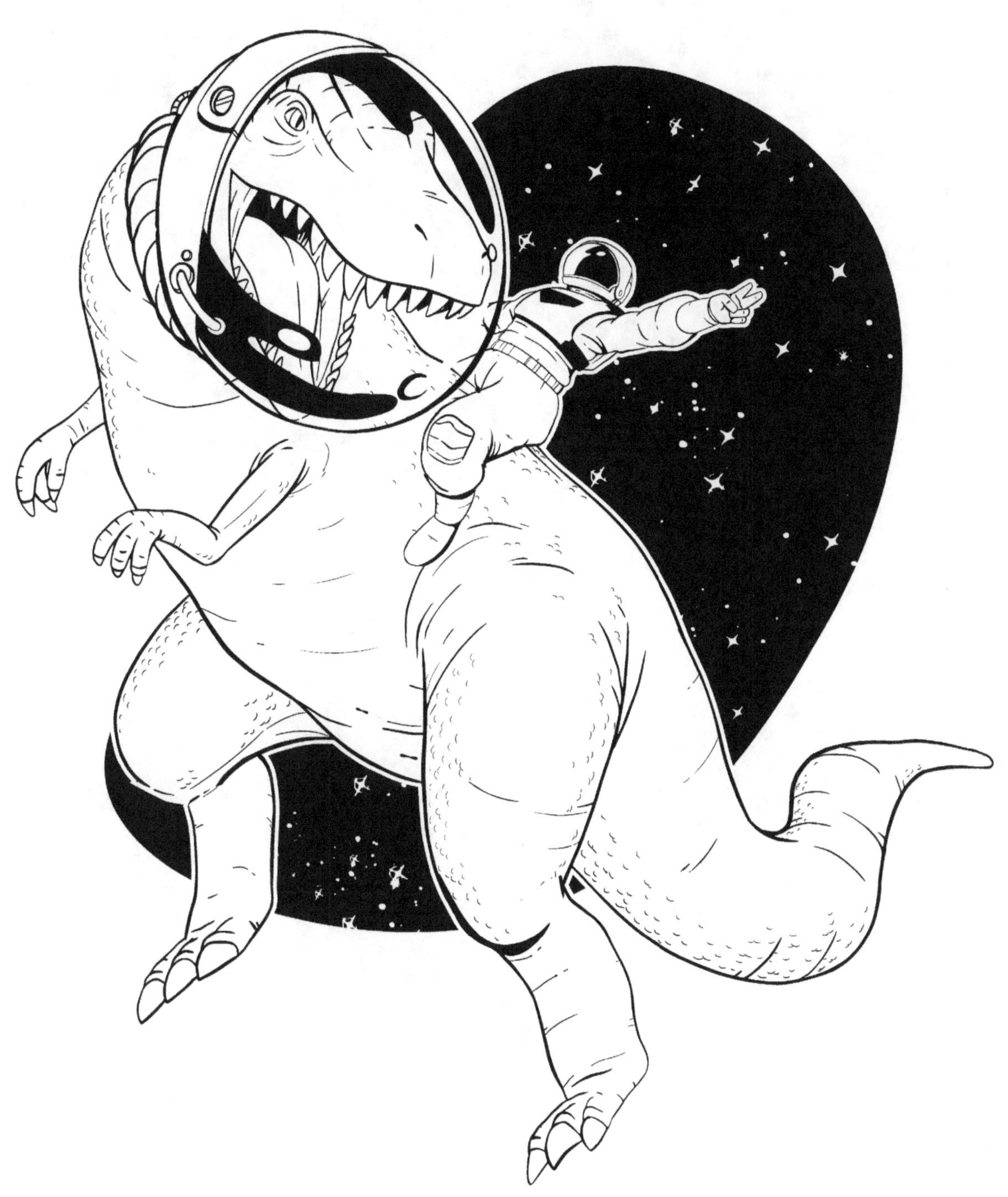

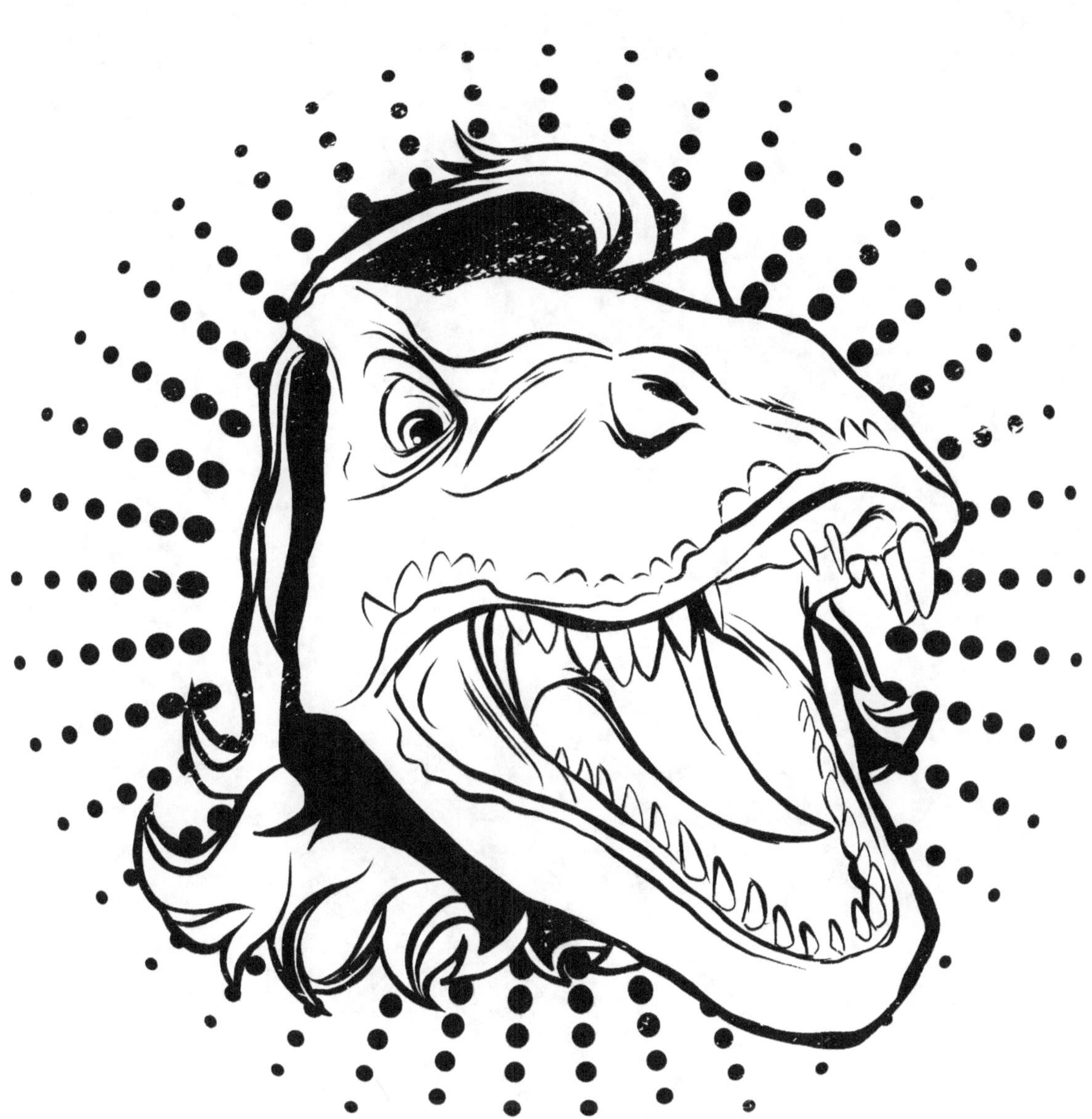

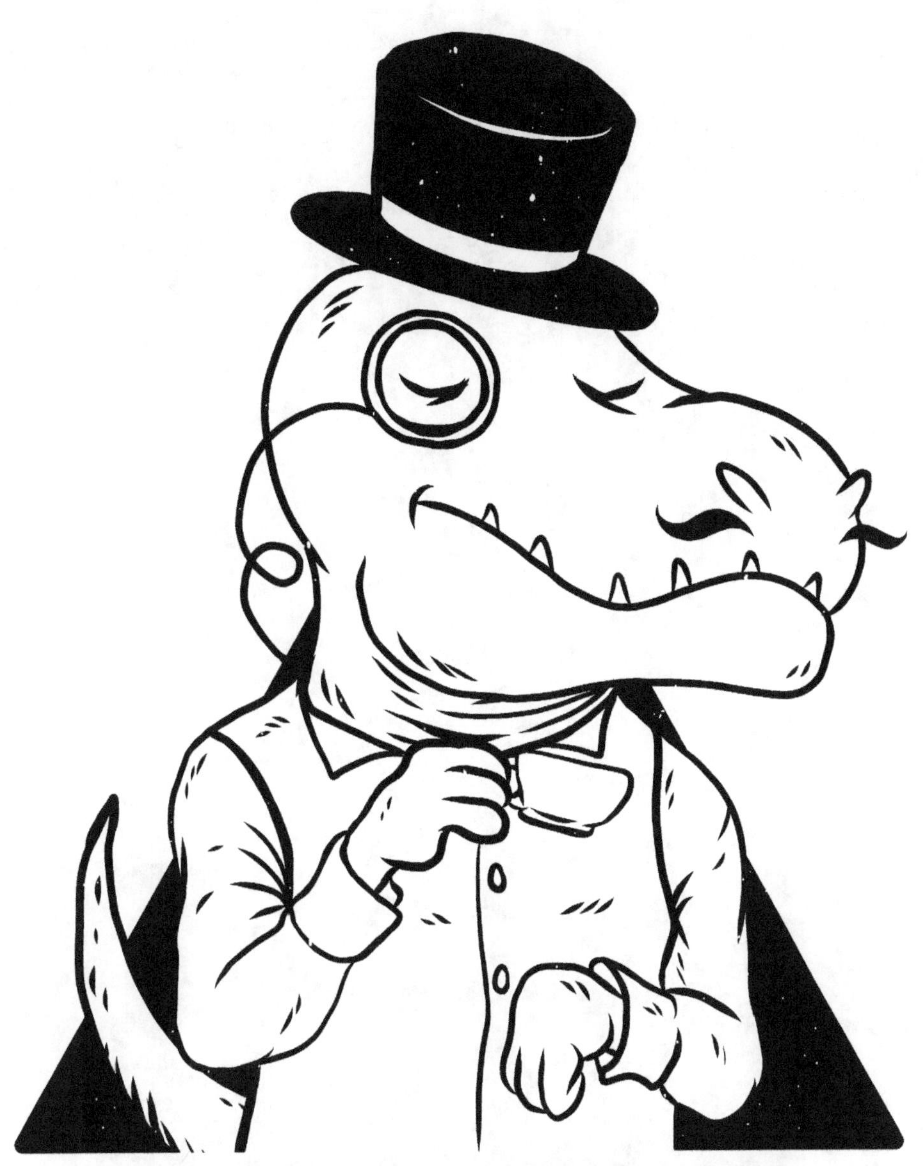

# TEAREX

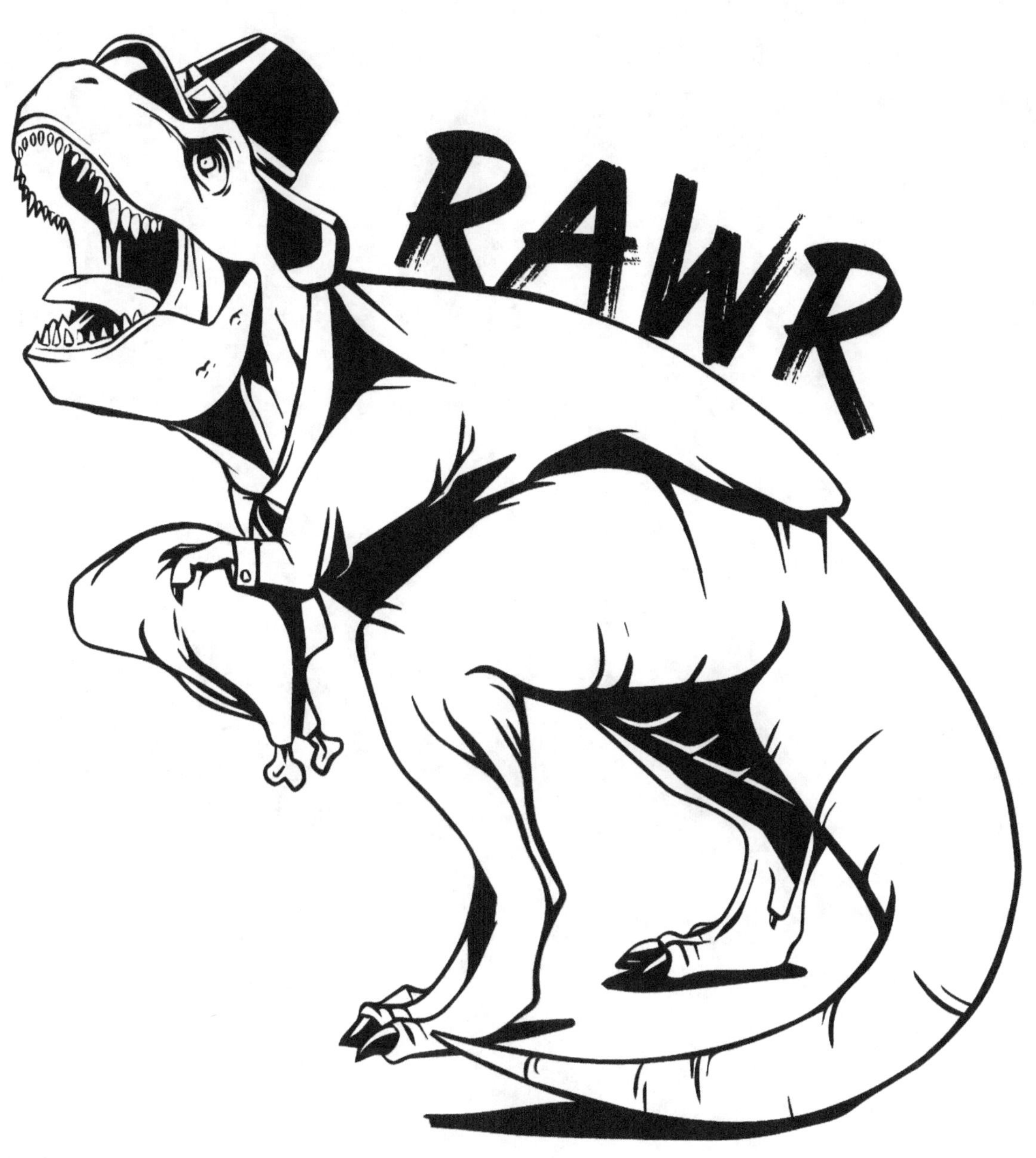

RAWR

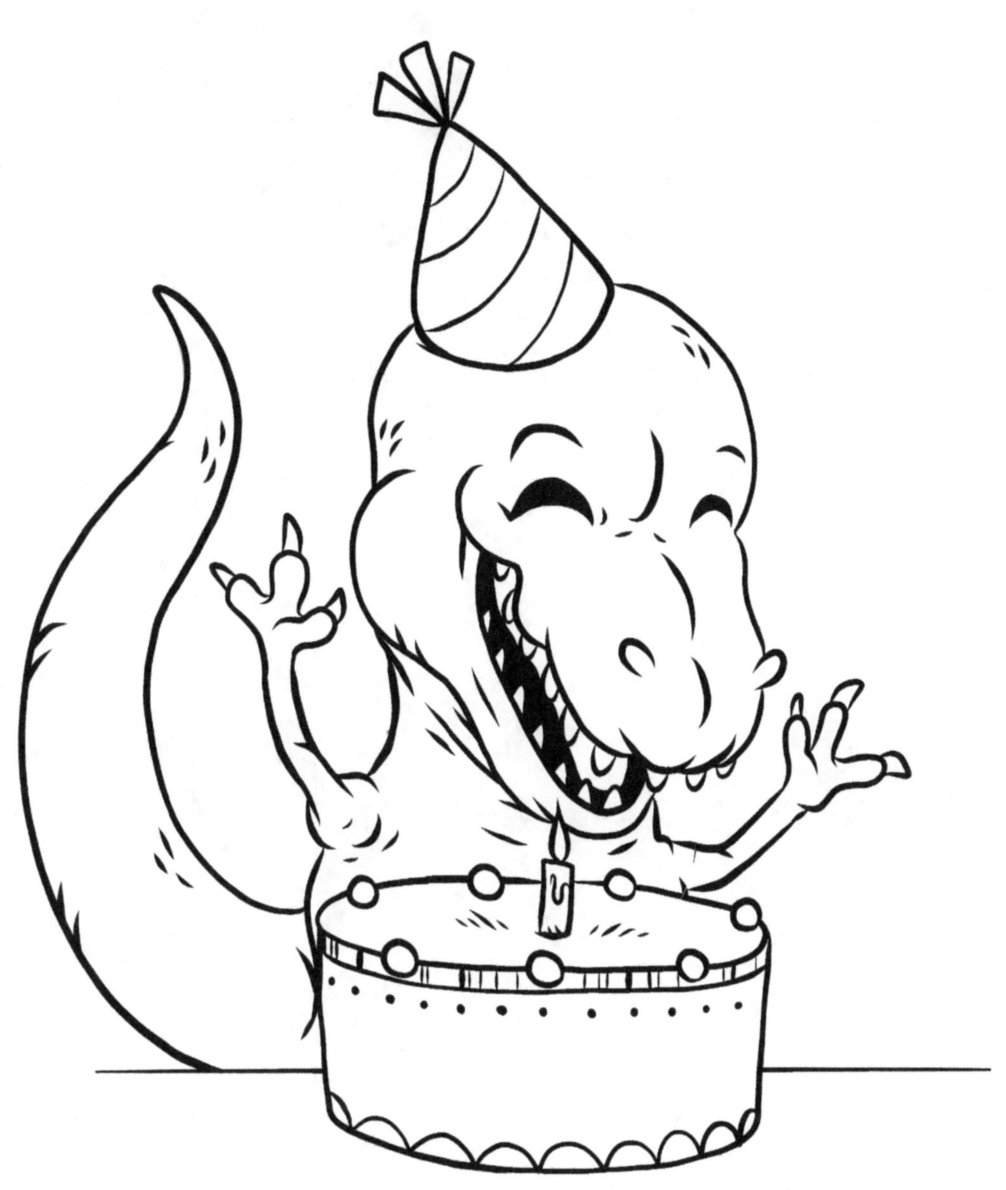

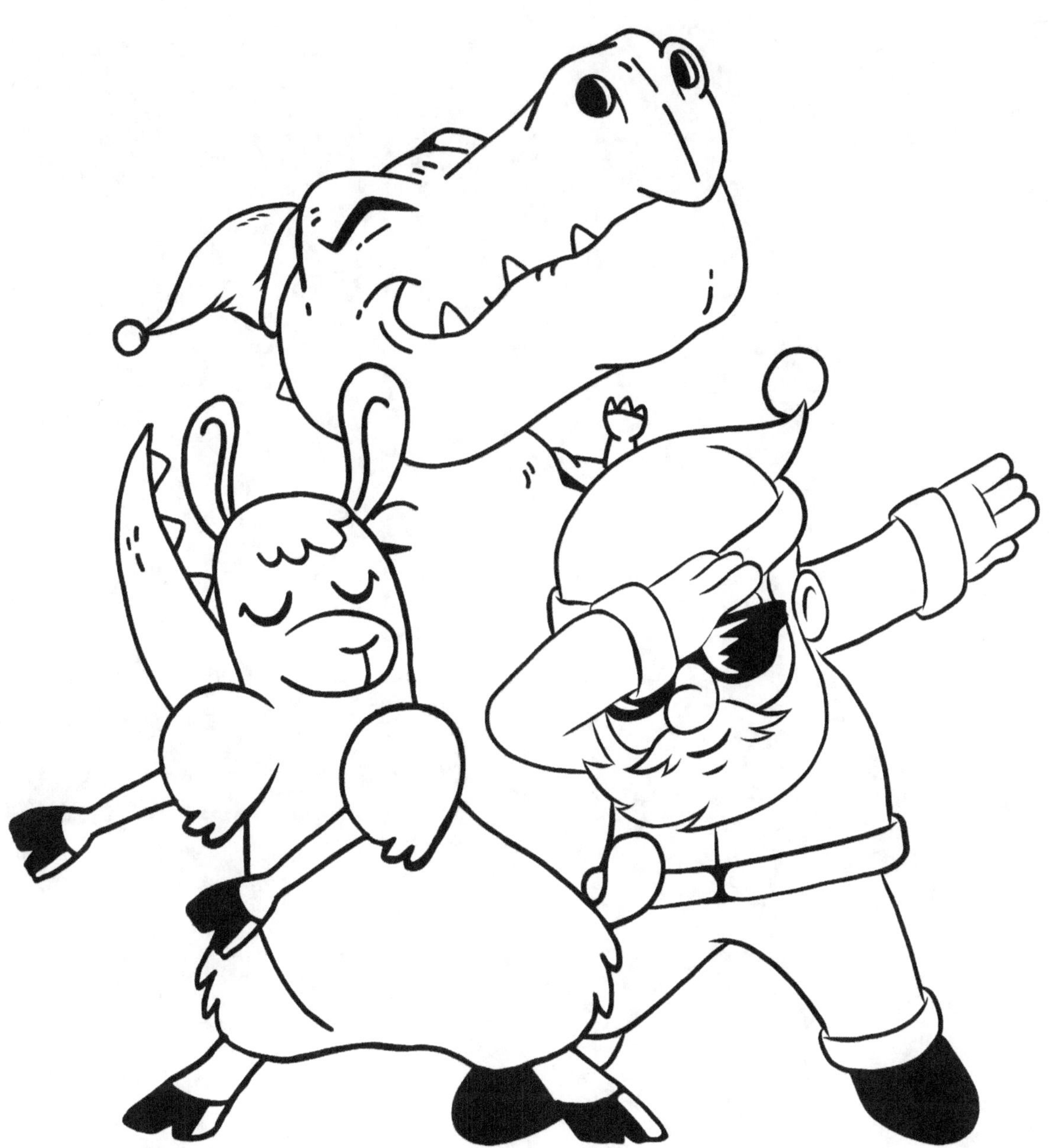

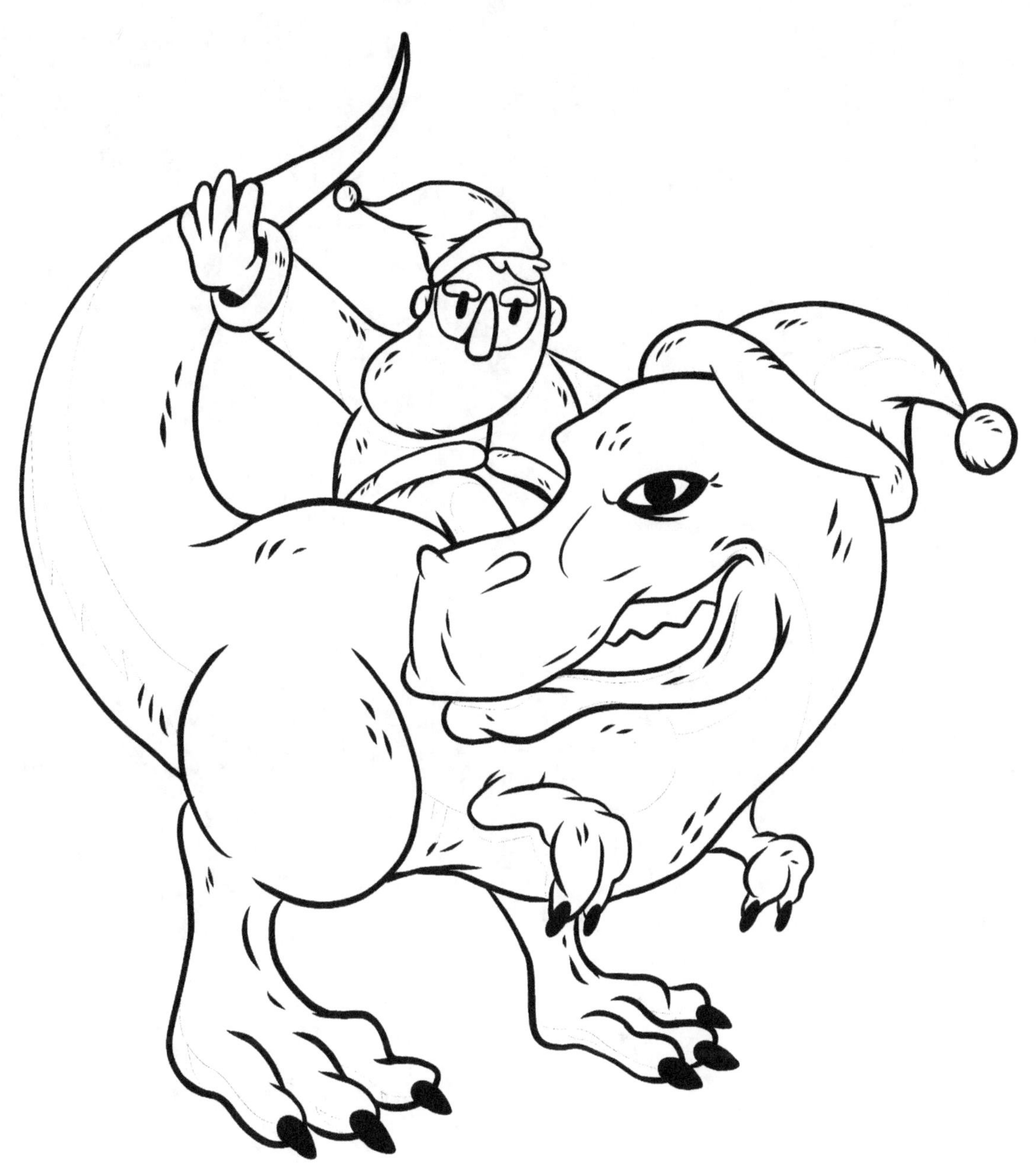

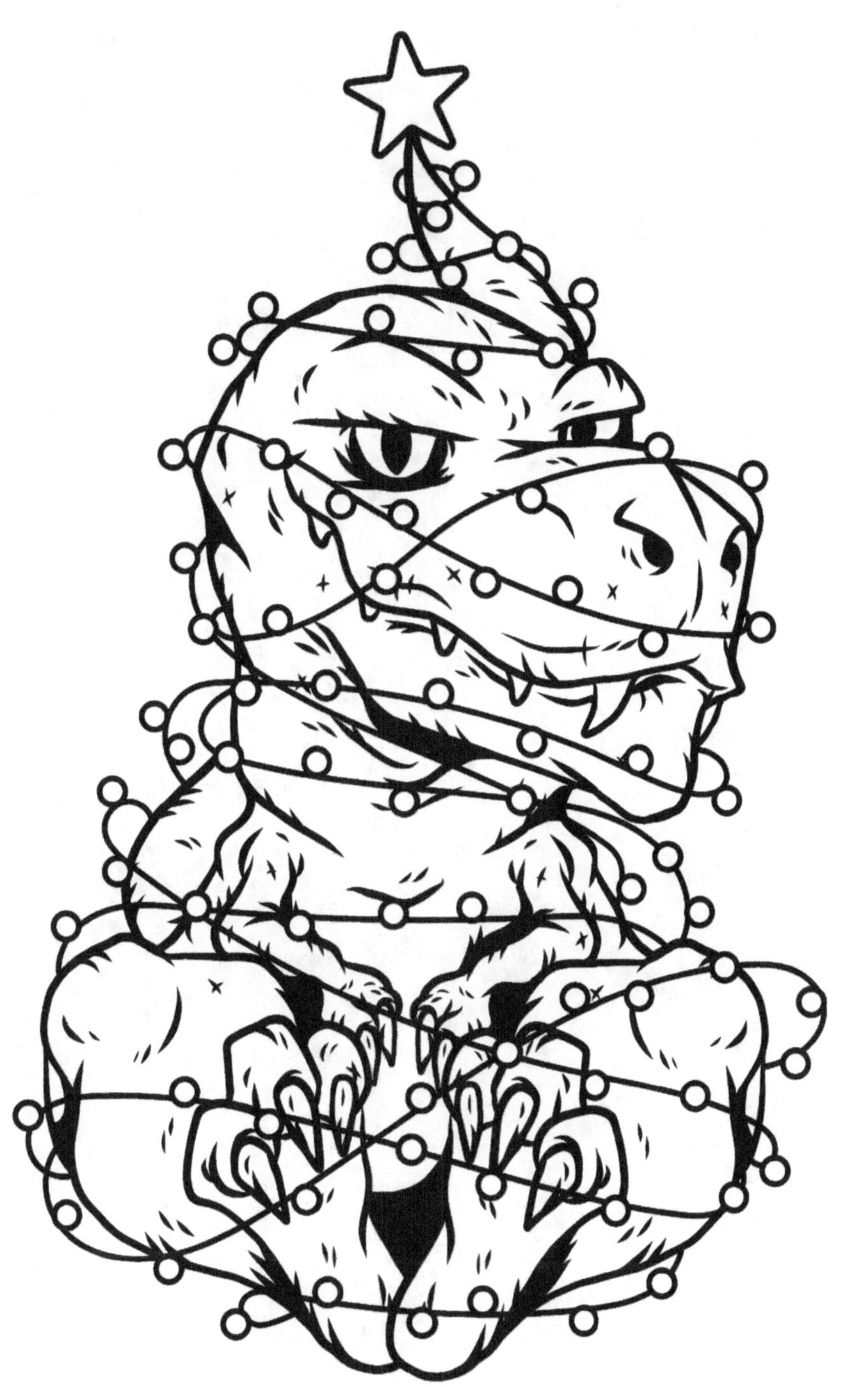

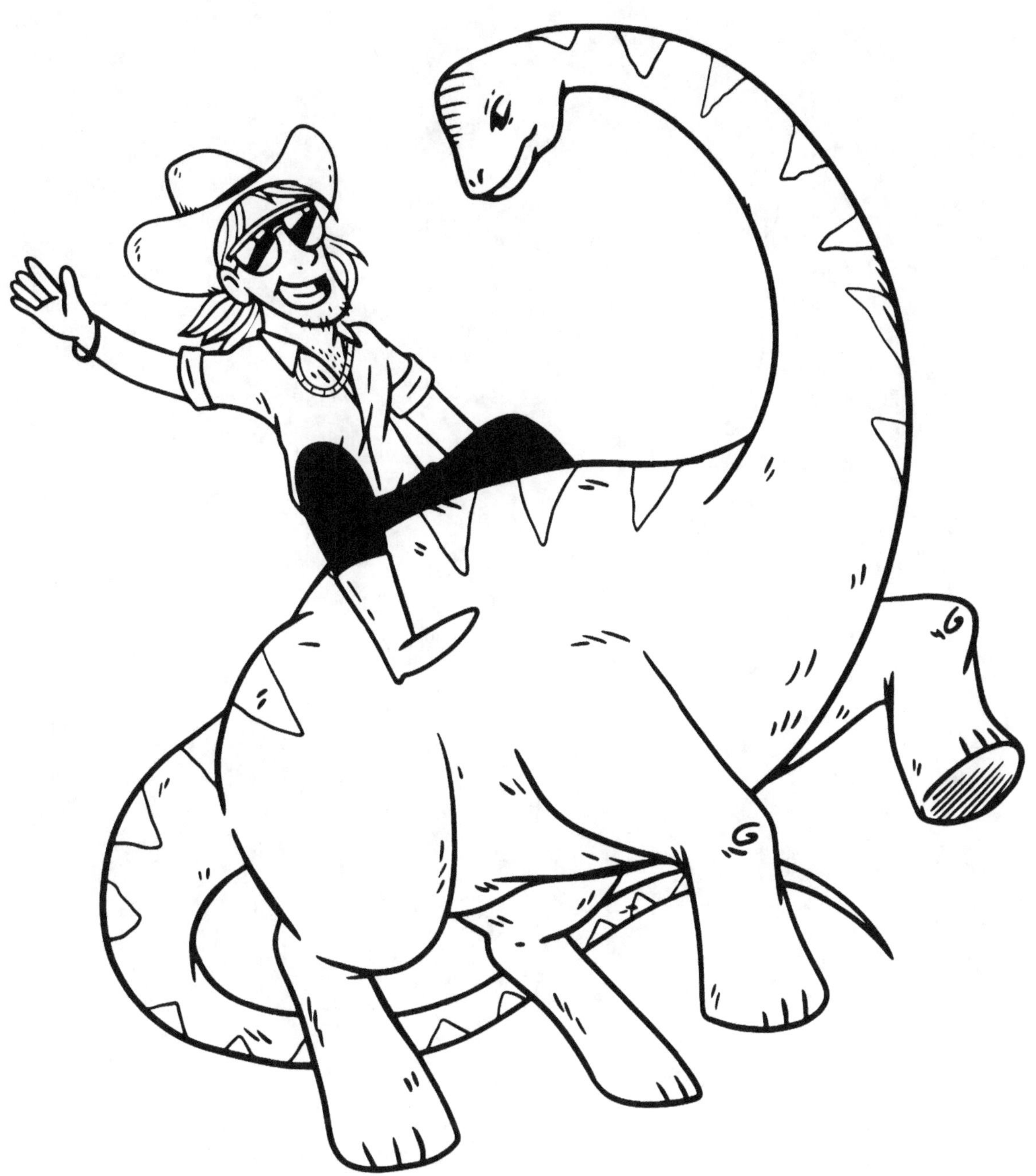